Romantic and Dream Vacations

WHITE STAR PUBLISHERS

Contents

TEXT
Jasmina Trifoni

EDITORIAL COORDINATION
Laura Accomazzo

GRAPHIC LAYOUT
Stefania Costanzo

A fairy tale castle or a tent in the desert?

Le voyage à la façon anglaise or 'journey in the English manner,' was what the French of the late 19th century called the romantic sojourn enjoyed by young British couples in the sun of the French Riviera, which runs from Nice to Menton. For the French, this was a strange thing. But for young British honeymooners, spending a few weeks in a small boarding house overlooking the sea and taking in the colors and scents of the Mediterranean was nothing less than an adventure – not only because in those days trips were long, tiring, and full of unforeseen events, but also and above all because what they called a honeymoon was a new marvelous way to begin married life.

Although the term 'honeymoon' dates to the time of the ancient Babylonians, to whom it meant the first month after the wedding – apparently because in their time the custom was for newlyweds to drink hydromel, a beverage made with fermented honey that has aphrodisiacal properties – romantic vacations as we understand them today are a recent invention, credit for which must be given to the loyal subjects of the austere Queen Victoria. In her era, their favorite honeymoon destination was France, a sort of promised land of passion (after all, English-speaking people used, and still use, the term 'French kiss' for the most amorous kiss of all), followed by the most languid and artistic places in Italy – from Venice and Tuscany to the Gulf of Naples.

More than 100 years have passed since those early timid journeys, and now it is considered quite odd if one does not go on a honeymoon after one's wedding. Furthermore, it is no longer necessary to take this romantic trip in the month that married life officially begins; today any occasion is good for a vacation for two. A couple can take off together to get to know each other better and to see how things turn out, or to take a break and enjoy each other's company far from everybody and everything, or again, to celebrate love in a dream-like setting, or even to try to save a relationship, hoping that it doesn't become a nightmare.

As for the destination, the sky's the limit. This is why we decided to begin this book on romantic vacations in places far, far away. So we will go straight to French Polynesia, first as a tribute to the French – so intrinsically passionate and *amoureux* – who colonized these jewels in the South Seas, and secondly, because Bora Bora is universally considered the most beautiful and romantic island in the world. What's more, our aim is to make you dream, and in a big way, about all the continents, both famous places (frequented by celebrities for trysts) and secret ones, from the white beaches of fantastic tropical islands in the Caribbean and Indian Ocean to the equally white snow in the world's most popular mountain destinations, from cities full of art and peaceful country

A love story
for every romantic destination

villages in the dear Old World, to the wild but no less fascinating ones in the Amazon forests and great African parks. You may choose from among the seductive lure of places that served as settings for great love stories, such as Romeo and Juliet's Verona, or Agra, in the India of the *Thousand and One Nights* with its fabulous Taj Mahal, the most astounding monument a man has ever built for his beloved. Depending on your taste and inclination you can choose to be carried away by the idea of a contemplative vacation in spring, during the cherry blossom season in Kyoto, the ancient capital of the mysterious Japan of the geishas; take a trip as adventurous as it is romantic in the magical world of ice in Lapland; sleep in a luxury tent on Ayers Rock, in the red center of Australia, or stay in the labyrinth of spectacular canyons in the western United States.

In our dreamy book, we have tried to offer you a place that will rouse enthusiasm about a trip for two. Are you gourmets? Then there is a getaway in the French region of Champagne where you can discover vineyards and caves with the sexiest bubbles on our planet. Do you love being pampered? Then there is no better place than Thailand, where you can indulge in voluptuous massages for just the two of you. And should you opt for a vacation on a boat – which, be warned, is the most relentless test of love – you can either go on a cruise in a caique or a schooner along the Turkish coast or among the Caribbean islands. Or you can sail down the Nile in a *dahabiyya*, the traditional ancient boat that made Flaubert fall in love with Egypt. This book will anticipate the emotions that you will feel while living in the desert among the dunes of Namibia or the infinite expanses of salt in Atacama, Chile, or again while becoming acquainted with such exotic cultures as those of the Maya or the Buddhist monks in Bhutan, the country where life is based on the concept of shared happiness. It will also give you some original ideas on how to make your vacation truly unique, whether you decide to get married in front of a blazing sunset on the Greek island of Santorini, or give her the engagement ring during your flight over a heart-shaped coral reef in Australia's Great Barrier Reef.

Since God is in the details, as the great architect Mies van der Rohe once stated, we have selected a special resort for each of the destinations – a boutique hotel, boat or even a king-sized bed under a star-studded sky – one that we feel will be the 'perfect nook' for a romantic dream vacation. In other words, here you have everything needed to imagine – and organize – the most enticing vacation in your life, be it an official honeymoon or merely a weekend of passion. What remains for you to decide on is a small but fundamental detail: the person with whom you who will share this experience.

2 / 3 - A safari at dawn in the Masai Mara to hear the heartbeat of Africa.

8 / 9 - The Maldives, a paradise (consisting of 99% water) for couples.

Bora Bora
French Polynesia

10 - Even the first view of Bora Bora from an airplane window is overwhelming. With its crystal clear lagoon, blinding white sand, and bright green vegetation, the island is, in fact, considered the world's most beautiful. Once you see the luxurious Four Seasons Resort, you will wish that your vacation may never end.

11 - 2385-foot Mt. Otemanu is the tallest peak on Bora Bora. Along with Mt. Pahia, it is what remains of a volcano that dominated the island millions of years ago.

For the Polynesians it is the *Vava'i*, 'the first-born,' created by the god Ta'aroa. And though it is not a question of genealogy, even for all the others – from James Cook, who arrived here in 1777, to the thousands and thousands of present-day tourists – Bora Bora is the 'first' in beauty in the whole world.

It is simply perfect, the archetype of the dream island, even in its geographical features and shape, which lie in that part of the legendary South Seas that history assigned to French colonists. And its 14 or so square miles of surface area are the result of a volcanic eruption that took place 3 million years ago. The island is still dominated by two black lava peaks, Otemanu and Pahia, which from a distance look like fairy-tale castles, and by lush and fragrant vegetation. Encircling the island is the famous turquoise lagoon 'held captive' by a necklace composed of *motu*, islets of pearl-colored sand that emerge from the barrier reef, which is likewise a jewel with its spectacular coral and 700 species of fish.

The largest *motu* on Bora Bora now has an airport, while luxury resorts have been established on most of the others. Each of these consists of a series of *fares*, typical Polynesian bungalows with palm leaf roofs, as well as exclusive *fare piloti*. The latter are deeply romantic bungalows standing on stilts over the water of the lagoon with windows offering a 'cropped' view of the sea below and a private terrace suspended over it. All the resorts are magnificent and compete with each other in offering unforgettable experiences, including organizing weddings in the most relaxed Polynesian style, accompanied by traditional dances and a profusion of flowers as well as 'peccadillos.'

Of these, couples in love will especially appreciate the ones at the Four Seasons Bora Bora, situated on the splendid Motu Tehotu, which offers them, among other things, a very special treat when they wake up. Here the sumptuous breakfast, with its tropical flavors, arrives by sea, conveyed on a *tiparua*, a typical double-keel canoe, by two Polynesians, their heads wrapped in hibiscus garlands, who announce its arrival by blowing into an ancient musical instrument made out of a seashell.

With such a beginning, every day spent at Bora Bora cannot but be perfect, whether you spend it in utter relaxation on the beach (you must go to Motu Tapu, a paradise that holds the record as the most photographed small island in the South Seas) or engaged in a pleasurable *tour de force* of land and water activities. The latter range from adventures in a kayak to cruises on a catamaran at sunset, or snorkeling and enjoying special experiences such as swimming with gigantic rays or feeding the harmless local sharks.

12 - It is impossible to determine whether Bora Bora is more marvelous on land or under water. Yet it certainly would be a pity not to engage in some adventurous diving in order to observe the multicolored and richly populated barrier reef.

12 / 13 - Watching the pink whipray – a fish endemic to Polynesia – move so elegantly in the transparent and shallow waters of the Bora Bora lagoon is a mesmerizing experience.

On land it is worthwhile taking a hike to the coconut palm plantations and the forest, then on to the peaks, or else becoming acquainted with Polynesian culture by exploring the *marae*, the ancient sacred stone temples that dot the coastline. Or again, you can spend some time shopping, because a vacation in Polynesia is also the right occasion to give your loved one a piece of jewelry adorned with precious local pearls, whose iridescent color ranges from light grey to coal-black while reflecting and amplifying all the sensations of the most beautiful island in the world. Forever.

Vanua Levu

Fiji

The South Seas syndrome is an illness that should be listed in medical books. Those who go to the Fiji Islands and feel the urge to stay there forever know it very well. Consisting of around 330 volcanic and coralline islands, the archipelago offers visitors white beaches bordered by palm trees and lagoons that are true to the romantic stereotype of *Blue Lagoon*, the movie that caused an entire generation to dream.

Most people would like to be shipwrecked – as Tom Hanks was in *Castaway*, one of the many blockbusters shot here – on one of its rocks and spend their time from now until eternity swimming and diving while exploring and enjoying its labyrinthine coral reef, the third largest in the world. And rather than being a nuisance, it is a pleasant surprise to get caught in a sudden shower and seek refuge among the forests, the volcanic peaks and the bucolic landscapes of the islands in order to enjoy the hospitality of the locals, who are always ready to offer visitors a bowl of *kava*, the traditional Melanesian drink and symbol of brotherhood concocted from red pepper roots.

In the 19th century, sailors from the West described the Melanesian people as "the most barbarous race on earth." They may have been right because cannibalism was commonly practiced among them in that time. Nowadays, on the other hand, the Fiji Tourist Office has coined a motto for the archipelago that could not be truer: "Fiji, where happiness finds you." And here, one of the 'creators of happiness' who deserves honorable mention is Jean-Michel Cousteau, the son of the legendary explorer of the depths of the sea, who, on the island of Vanua Levu, founded the most luxurious and ethical eco-resort in the archipelago, with 25 private *bure* – traditional local bungalows with palm-leaf roofs – immersed in a coconut tree plantation and a few steps away from a stunningly colored sea.

While it is wonderful to have nothing to do and be taken for a picnic on the idyllic islet of Naviavia, a few hundred yards from the resort (and which can be reserved for the exclusive use of a couple for a full day), or be pampered by the traditional ritual of a massage with coconut oil, it is impossible not to be tempted by the many activities offered here, all

14 / 15 - An aerial view of the Cousteau Resort at Vanua Levu, whose owner is the son of Jean-Jacques, the legendary ocean explorer. Guests can choose from a myriad of activities, but snorkeling or diving in the spectacular coral reef gardens alongside a marine biologist is definitely a must.

of which are unforgettable. You can – or rather, you must – go snorkeling or diving in the coral gardens with an oxygen tank, accompanied by the resort's marine biologist. It is worth your while to abandon the beaches for a few hours to explore the island's luxuriant nature or go to the main city, Savusavu, with its picturesque market, where local colors merge with the scent of Indian and Chinese spices brought here by their respective communities of immigrants. In the evening, happiness arrives in the form of the social *lovo*, the typical Fijian banquet accompanied by a highly sensual local dance, the *meke*, as well as moments of perfect intimacy, such as a romantic dinner for two on a small pier suspended over a transparent lagoon. There is only one word for this experience – and not only because it sounds like *lovo* – and that is 'love.'

16 - During low tide you can go on foot from Vanua Levu to the deserted islet of Naviavia. Witnessing a multicolored sunset reflected in the ocean here is a marvelous experience.

17 *top* - The resort's massage studio is located in a *bure*, a typical Fijian palm-wood structure, where you can enjoy a traditional coconut oil massage while being caressed by the sea breeze.

17 *bottom* - A romantic candlelit dinner on the resort pier, which juts out into the blue lagoon of magical Savusavu Beach.

Vava'u
Tonga

18 - From an airplane window each island in the Vava'u chain looks like a chunk of paradise. While this aerial view is satisfying, it is a mere hint of what is in store for you. The archipelago consists of 50 islands in a subaquatic coral reef system displaying an incredible array of colors, a sight most fully enjoyed from a sailboat.

19 - The sea at Vava'u is the only place in the world where – from July to November – you can enjoy the fantastic experience of swimming with whales that migrate here from Antarctica to give birth and wean their young.

Tu i Malila passed on to a better world in 1965 at the venerable age of 188, practically becoming a national monument. He was in actual fact the giant tortoise that Captain James Cook gave to the king of Tonga when he landed on the archipelago, in July 1777, at the precise moment when the court was celebrating the annual Inasi feast in honor of the fruit that this bounteous land has given its people. Perhaps partly thanks to his kind gift, Cook – who elsewhere on his travels in the South Seas had had to deal with rather aggressive natives – was received with all due honors and thus named this particular kingdom the 'Friendly Islands.' Although it was 'plain sailing' for him, later visitors did not have the same good fortune; until a century ago, cannibalism was common in Tonga (in the mid-19th century, in fact, all members of one American crew ended up in the cauldron save a certain Elisabeth Mosey because a court dignitary had fallen in love with her and desired her as his bride). Indeed, Tonga is the only archipelago in the Pacific that no one has succeeded in colonizing.

Now there is nothing to worry about, however; all this belongs to the past. Today the Kingdom of Tonga heartily welcomes visitors to its enchanting land, where they can spend their vacation, however brief, on one of its four groups of islands. Among these, first prize goes to Vava'u, a group of about 50 islets (very few of which

are inhabited) that dot a barrier reef system with a sea of incredible nuances of color, amazing biodiversity, perfect visibility up to a depth of 130 feet, and, above all, with the well deserved fame of being the best destination for a sailboat vacation in the Pacific.

It goes without saying that the best way to enjoy Vava'u is to sail among the islands by renting a boat along with a crew from the New Zealand charter company, The Moorings. The excursion usually lasts 10 days and the itinerary will let you visit paradises such as Kapa, Kenutu, Mounu, and Nuku, each with villages in which you can get a taste of the local culture and see the coastal caves and magnificent white sand beaches bordered by coconut palms, and pretend to be Robinson Crusoe on uninhabited islets in the middle of spectacular lagoons. While it is all too easy to feel the urge to play castaway for a few days on a deserted island, taking in breathtaking sunsets, tropical fruit and love, the marvelous archipelago also offers thrilling activities for couples, from snorkeling among the barrier reefs to swimming with mantas, whose movements are comparable only to those of ballet dancers. And from July to November, here, and only here, you can take part in the truly memorable experience of swimming with whales that have traveled more than 5000 miles from Antarctica to give birth and wean their young.

Kaua'i
USA

Forget Waikiki Beach and the hordes of tourists with their gaudy floral shirts. The shirts, in any case, are made in China. You can also ignore the surfers' 'big day' on the island of Maui; their parties are not exactly the kind of event you would want to attend if you already have a partner. In short, skip – or better, fly over – the most famous 'American' Hawaiian Islands and land in what is the best kept secret (at least for the time being) in the archipelago: Kaua'i. The fact that this island is relatively unknown can be seen in its landscape, which must be explored slowly and with the right dose of fatigue, whether you venture onto panoramic paths along vertiginous basalt cliffs along the Na Pali Coast in the northern part of the island, or into the island's very heart, the spectacular Waimea Canyon, which is 12 miles long and up to 2800 feet deep. Testimony of the romantic nature of the island is the flower that has been chosen as its symbol, the *hau*, a hibiscus whose petals change color several times in a single day: pale yellow in the morning, orange at midday, and dark red at sunset, when it prepares for the night. And with regard to romantic sport, there is the Coconut Coast, a soft belt of golden sand that encloses the entire southern section of the island; in 1961 this was the site of many scenes in the saccharine movie, *Blue Hawaii*, starring the 'grinder' Elvis Presley, who stirred the hearts of an entire generation of girls (as well as former girls). History itself shows that there is something strange and incomprehensible about Kaua'i. It was the first of the Hawaiian Islands to be colonized, around AD 500, but to this day, at least among the larger islands, it is the one in which human impact is least noticeable. The inhabitants of Kaua'i swear that what keeps 'invaders' at bay are *menehune*, the disrespectful elves of Hawaiian tradition and mythology. But the rational explanation is that the wild, almost primeval appearance of the island is indebted to a strict law that prohibits the construction of buildings taller than a palm tree. While there are too many skyscrapers to count in Honolulu, here there are only a handful of resorts on the seaside, all of which are exclusive and environment-friendly. Of these, the place of honor belongs to the St. Regis Princeville, renowned for its subtle elegance and perfect blend of architecture and landscape. What is certain is that Kaua'i has that extra something that makes people fall in love. But this becomes evident only if you venture as far as Fern Grotto, which is enveloped in ferns and which the ancients believed was the home of Lono, the god of fertility. If you're looking for a magic place where you can give her the engagement ring...well, you've found it.

20 / 21 - A romantic sunset over the St. Regis Princeville Resort and the tall, dramatic cliffs overlooking the ocean along the wild coast of Na Pali.

20

The Blue Mountains
Australia

22 - Secluded, extremely luxurious, yet highly ecological, Emirates Wolgan Valley Resort is the ideal setting for a couple to enjoy on their own the wild natural setting of the vast UNESCO-protected Blue Mountains area.

23 - Only two hours by automobile from Sydney, the sandstone formations of the Three Sisters are the iconic 'calling card' of the Blue Mountains.

The discovery of the Wollemia pine (*Wollemia nobilis*) has been called the greatest botanical find of the 20th century. Thought to have become extinct along with dinosaurs, this majestic conifer appeared as if by magic to the naturalist David Noble during an excursion in the canyons and forests of the Blue Mountains in September 1994. This was a remarkable and incredible stroke of luck, considering the fact that these mountains in densely populated New South Wales are the most accessible and popular natural paradise in Australia. Indeed the canyon in which the discovery was made is only 93 miles from a metropolis such as Sydney. It must be said, however, that the Blue Mountains are a land of miracles. First of all, they were named after the surreal color of the landscape during Australian summer, when high temperatures cause the release of microscopic particles of the fragrant oil in eucalyptus trees, which, upon contact with sunlight, produce a chemical reaction that leads to refraction in the ultraviolet spectrum.

In autumn and spring, on the other hand, a mysterious climatic phenomenon, the so-called phantom waterfalls, occurs here when, under certain humid conditions, a cloud of spray traveling at a speed of 65 feet per second plunges; the falls are nearly 1100 yards wide and may last from a few minutes to a few hours, after which they suddenly disappears.

With a surface area of over a million hectares and protected by 8 different reserves, the Blue Mountains boast landscapes of splendid pinnacles and canyons shaped by millions of years of erosion, waterfalls (which, unlike those mentioned above, are perennial), and mystical forests dominated by a great number of eucalyptus species that conceal a vast network of caves waiting to be explored. As for its fauna, among many other animals there are 52 species of mammals, with a predominance of grey kangaroos, wallabies, koalas, and wombats.

The mountains have a formidable cultural heritage as well since they have been inhabited for millennia by Aborigines, who have left sites rich in rock carvings. Their proximity to Sydney makes them an ideal spot to spend the weekend on all kinds of activities. For those who love exciting sports, there is rock climbing.Those who prefer a romantic atmosphere can enjoy a ride on the scenic cog railway or take a hike for two among enchanting valleys, or even book a first-row ticket for one of the concerts performed by members of the Sydney Philharmonic Orchestra, which are held in the fascinating clearings. Then again, if you would like to spend a few days far from everything and everybody, the Blue Mountains have many resorts in wild natural settings. The most remote and luxurious of these is the Emirates Wolgan Valley Resort & Spa, which consists of 40 suites, each with its own private pool and overlooking magnificent scenery reminiscent of *Jurassic Park*. What's more, it is a short distance from the 'secret' canyon that contains 100 specimens of the prehistoric *Wollemia nobilis*.

Ayers Rock

Australia

24 - For the Aborigines, Ayers Rock is Uluru, that is, the 'Red Center' that is bound to their myth of creation and for this reason the area should be visited with due respect. Longitude 131°, standing at the gateway to the dual World Heritage listed wilderness, offers immersion in the Australian outback, a true sense of stillness and beauty in this desert landscape, rich in cultural heritage and timeless history.

25 - An excursion on camelback to the sacred Aboriginal sites in the Uluru-Kata Tjuta National Park is especially thrilling at sunset, when the landscape is ablaze with magical colors.

In the beginning was *Tjukurpa*, or Dreamtime. The Earth was flat and empty, with neither light nor darkness, as nature waited for the divine ancestral spirits to impart form and life to it. It was they who created Uluru, the 'Red Center,' the mountain that would witness all subsequent events. This is the myth of creation according to the Anangu Aboriginals, for whom Uluru – or Ayers Rock, as it was later named by the explorer William Gosse, who 'discovered' it – is the loftiest spiritual symbol. Now they own and manage the national park that protects what, for all other people, is the principal natural monument in the Australian outback, and try to discourage people from climbing to the top, which they consider a profanation of their most sacred site.

1142 feet high and with a circumference of 5.8 miles, this massive sandstone monadnock rises up over the desert, but, like an iceberg, most of its bulk is hidden underground. What is visible, however, is extraordinary. This huge sedimentary rock was formed about 300 million years ago and is literally encrusted with ferrous inclusions, which thanks to oxidation, are responsible for its special orange and rust color. At dawn and dusk, as Ayers Rock is ablaze with glowing red hues, the rising

and setting sun and the sky produce a chromatic spectacle that does not seem of this planet. The scenery generates the greatest thrill precisely in these brief moments, much as it bewitched the seasoned traveler and English author Bruce Chatwin, who devoted one of his most famous books, *The Songlines*, to Uluru and Aboriginal myths. Chatwin admired the Anangu quite a bit and wrote that they move about the Earth with a light step; the less they take from the Earth, the less they need to give back.

Consequently, one must enjoy the dream of the ancestral land of the Anangu with these words in mind, respecting the regulations they have imposed on the sacred sites in the national park – including the Uluru monolith and nearby Mount Olga (or The Olgas), the 'foreign' name of the craggy pinnacles of Kata Tjuta, or Many Heads. A walk through the dramatic Walpa Gorge whilst learning of the region's remarkable geological history is an enlightening, must-do experience.

In line with the spiritual and ecological philosophy of the Anangu people, the most ethical and romantic accommodation here is a luxury campsite, Longitude 131°, whose name is a tribute to the geographical coordinates of Ayers Rock.

This is a zero-impact resort that has imported the concept of 'glamping,' a fusion of glamor and camping, to the 'new' continent. Each tent pays homage to an early explorer or pioneer, and all have a glass wall with a fine view of the monolith so that guests can wake up to the thrill of watching the sun rise over the ancient landscape.

26 - Longitude 131° takes its name from the coordinates of Ayers Rock. The strong, resilient presence of Uluru is with guests almost every minute of their stay, whether lying in bed, dining at the Dune House, swimming in the pool or sightseeing atop a sand dune.

27 - The contemporary and spacious interior of one of the magnificent tents. Each is dedicated to a European pioneer who explored this territory, with historical journals and objets d'art complemented by Indigenous artworks and artefacts, made by the local Anangu communities.

Hamilton Island

Australia

28 *top* - Whitehaven Beach is one of the most famous beaches in Australia. It is known for its 4 mile stretch of pure white silica sand.

28 *bottom* - Considered the most sophisticated and elegant resort in Australia, qualia on Hamilton Island is a unique Australian expression of world-class luxury, where everything has been meticulously considered to relax the mind and completely spoil the senses.

29 - During your vacation on the Whitsunday Islands you absolutely must take the romantic and extraordinarily panoramic flight in a tiny plane over the Great Barrier Reef.

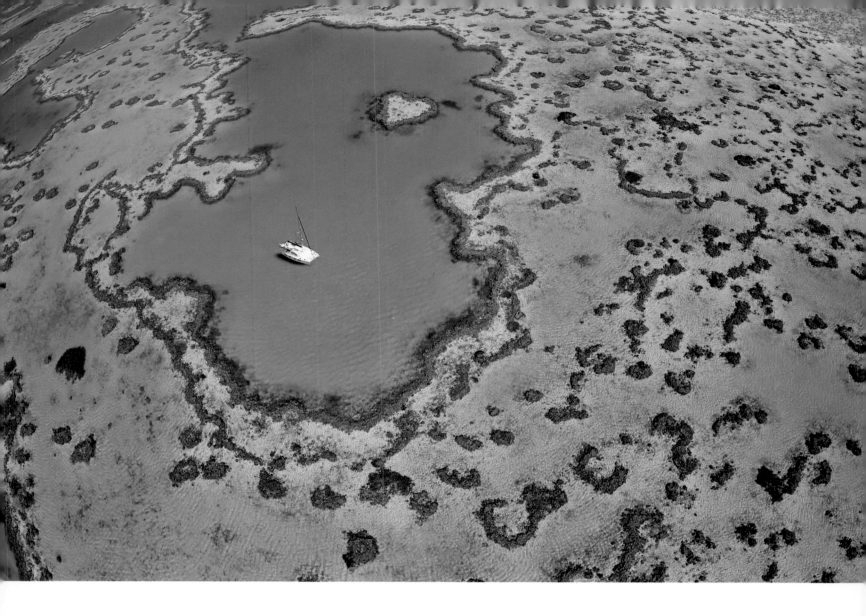

Heart Reef was discovered in 1975 by a Whitsunday Air pilot during a panoramic flight over the Great Barrier Reef. Since that time – and despite its rather modest size, a diameter of little more than 55 feet – this heart-shaped coral formation has become the romantic icon of Australia. Therefore, if during your vacation in Australia you should want to ask your sweetheart to marry you, here is a good piece of advice: book a scenic flight and, when you are over Hardy Lagoon exactly on a level with the Heart Reef and flying over this enchanting place, the pilot will nod, indicating that this is the right moment to give her the ring. The seaplane will then turn towards Hook Reef and Bait Reef and land on the turquoise sea before Whitehaven, the most beautiful beach in the world, for a picnic accompanied by a bottle of champagne. Arguably this might be a bit too schmaltzy, but you will be surprised at how many men have decided to enjoy this experience and have received 'yes' as an answer 100% of the time. On the other hand, extravagant gestures such as this may in fact become redundant during a vacation to the Whitsunday Islands, a group of 74 islands that lie at the very heart of the Great Barrier Reef.

Hamilton Island is the hub of that archipelago, and, with a surface area of only 1.9 square miles, constitutes an idyllic microcosm of tropical Australia. Here we have magnificent beaches, exhilarating natural surroundings where you can observe wallabies and koalas from up close and stay at qualia, the ultimate Australian luxury resort, which experts and enthusiastic guests have voted the best in the country. Owned by the legendary yachtsman and wine-grower Bob Oatley, qualia boasts 60 individual pavilions, some with private plunge pools, all nestled perfectly into the surrounding tropical bushland with breathtaking views. What is more, the concierge of this oasis of luxury and privacy can organize exciting activities for two throughout the archipelago, from sailboat trips to snorkeling and diving, as well as whale-watching tours, since from June to September the sea around the Great Barrier Reef serves as a sanctuary for these creatures.

And while Hamilton Island offers much in terms of stylish shopping and evening entertainment, each Whitsunday Island is a paradise in itself, which can be discovered along the Ngaro Sea Trail by following the tracks of the Aboriginals who first settled here, and which includes such destinations as South Molle Island, Hook Island, and Whitsunday, the largest in the archipelago. The islands are so close to each other that they can easily be reached between by boat, and all have well-marked trails most with facilities. From 220 yards to a little over 4 miles long, they lead to lovely stretches of rainforest, ancient rock carvings, and waterfalls. And, of course, to fantastic beaches. So, whether you arrive by seaplane (with your sweetheart wearing the ring) or canoe, marvelous Whitehaven Beach will be breathtaking; with its 98% silica sand glittering in the sun, like a million diamond rings.

One&Only Hayman Island
Australia

30 *top* - Covered with thick tropical vegetation, Hayman Island truly resembles an Eden reserved for the very few.

30 *bottom* - Literally a stone's throw from the splendid bedroom, the pool is an open invitation to a romantic evening swim.

31 - The white and turquoise beach umbrella (the same color as the sand and water) resembles a flag marking – for one day – exclusive ownership of magical Langford Island.

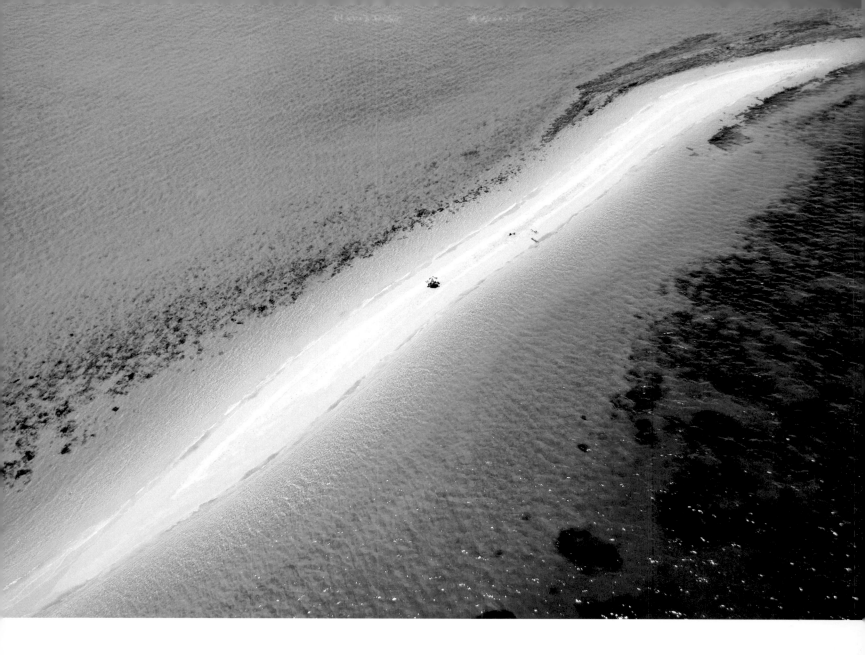

It is quite large, even for a member of such a robust species, and the colors of its iridescent skin range from turquoise to aquamarine, bright green to a delicate pinkish grey, accompanied by a network of thin yellow lines. Its thick lips look as though they have undergone plastic surgery. Some say that when it spots a beautiful female with a mask and fins, it sends kisses with those lips. This is the fish that Australians call Maori wrasse, whose permanent residence lies among the rocks, coral, and sea fans of Blue Pearl Bay, the most intimate and sensational 'natural address' on Hayman Island, at the northern border of the Whitsunday Islands in the Great Barrier Reef.

It goes without saying that Hayman Island itself is the most hospitable and astounding destination within the entire archipelago. There is much good luck in store for visitors to this tiny jewel 'mounted' on one of the most beautiful seas in the world that those fortunate enough to see the Maori wrasse at Blue Pearl Bay might decide that there is nothing more to desire in life, especially if they go there with their sweethearts. At best, they might still want to go for a romantic stroll on the long strip of white sand that is Langford Island, another incredible paradise a short distance from Hayman Island.

A vacation on Hayman Island is an absolute privilege. Discovered by Captain James Cook, it was a location destined to be famous, even among its many splendid

'sisters' in this archipelago. It received its present name in the late 19th century in honor of Thomas Hayman, the captain who, with his commander George Nares, was at the helm of the first ship that made the inaugural voyage down the Suez Canal followed by the extremely perilous circumnavigation of Antarctica. Much later, in 1947, the island was purchased by the Australian aviation pioneer Reginald Ansett, who, three years later, opened the famous Royal Hayman Hotel, which was immediately honored by a visit on the part of the British king and queen. Hayman Island, which has passed through several owners in the last 60 years, has gradually attained world-wide fame as an exclusive place for honeymoons as well as private meetings among power-wielders. (It was here, in 1995, in fact, that Tony Blair, the leader of the New Labour Party, met the Australian telecommunications magnate Rupert Murdoch to ask for – and obtain –support for his upcoming campaign in the United Kingdom). On July 1st 2014, the ultra-luxury private island resort and leader in hotel management, One&Only Resort, took over. The island is a dreamy refuge, in which everything is simply perfect – from the elegance of the suites to the paradisiacal gardens, the cuisine, the One&Only Spa, the gamut of seaplane excursions, and a host of tailor-made romantic activities, such as the underwater kisses of the Maori wrasse.

Lake Taupo
New Zealand

In 186 AD, the skies of Europe suddenly became red. The sole explanation for this phenomenon offered by ancient Roman chroniclers of the time was that it was a sign of the gods' wrath. Only many centuries later did it become clear that this terrifying sight was related to an incident that had occurred nearly simultaneously on the other side of the Earth, on the North Island of New Zealand. The so-called Taupo Eruption, an extremely violent one by the volcano bearing this name, drastically changed the features of this region and enlarged the size of Lake Taupo (already created many thousands of years earlier by the much greater Oruanui Eruption), forming a huge caldera later filled with water. Thus, due to the more recent eruption the lake became nearly an inland sea, now a marvelous natural paradise. The lower depths of the lake are still hot, so much so that only 50 years ago particularly intense geothermal activity created both a series of clefts emitting sulfuric vapors on the very thin layer of terrestrial crust on its northern shore, and craters of boiling mud. In any case, Lake Taupo is a warm

destination for many other reasons. It is a very sacred site for the Maori population. By Mine Bay, on the southern shore, a large rock face reveals a gigantic bas-relief representing Ngatoroirangi, the legendary Maori navigator who led his people to the heart of the island, along with a siren and the god of the South Wind, who helped them to achieve their goal. The lake is an awesome place for sports and entertainment, and offers possibilities for many romantic adventures. For example, you can go on a kayak or sailboat, on foot or by bicycle to see the stunning landscape, which includes snow-capped mountains and primeval forests, or you can try your hand at other activities that will really get your adrenalin going, such as sky diving (which you must do with your partner) or white-water rafting along the Waikato, the longest river in New Zealand.

Just before flowing into the lake, the Waikato creates the spectacle of the magnificent and incessantly photographed Huka Falls, after which the most luxurious and iconic lodge on the North Island has been named. Huka Lodge is perfect for a romantic vacation and has the same atmosphere

32 / 33 - Everything is ready for a romantic dinner for two on the jetty of Huka Lodge, the most iconic luxury resort on North Island, New Zealand. Down here the waters of the Waikato River flow peacefully among the vegetation, but a little way upstream, before hitting reaching Huka Falls, they are impetuous.

34 - The huge Mt. Ruapehu volcano dominates Tongariro National Park, a grand wild nature reserve holding a series of sites sacred to the indigenous Maori.

35 *top* - The courtship ritual of the Australasian gannets, seen here from the splendid cliff overlooking the ocean at Cape Kidnappers.

35 *bottom* - A thrilling helicopter ride provides a bird's-eye view of the crater of Mt. Ruapehu, which is 9176 feet high.

it did when it first opened in 1924 as an ideal spot for fly-fishing buffs. In fact, among its many guests have been the legendary aviator Charles Lindbergh and the American author James Michener, who in 1950 wrote part of the novel *Return to Paradise* there. Even if you are not interested in fishing, you can spend unforgettable days – and nights – here lulled by the relaxing sound of the river and enjoying the charming surrounding garden as well as the excellent cuisine (including a wine cellar with the best New Zealand labels). From Huka Lodge you can organize exciting adventures just for two, such as helicopter rides among the volcanic peaks in the Tongariro National Park or even fly as far as the dramatic marine vistas at Cape Kidnappers, which is home to the large protected colony of Australasian gannets.

Queenstown
New Zealand

One of the most magical locations in *The Hobbit: An Unexpected Journey*, the first movie in the world-famous trilogy, is Earnslaw Burn, a glacier with a series of waterfalls plunging from immense rock faces with a tremendous roar. Just a short distance from Queenstown, the town that New Zealanders have labeled the 'world capital of adventure,' are innumerable sites that served as settings for the six *Lord of the Rings* and *Hobbit* blockbusters. A guidebook with all their GPS coordinates has been published, and a tremendously popular sport among tourists is to go treasure hunting for fantastical experiences in the countryside.

Peter Jackson, the New Zealander director of these movies, once stated that ever since his adolescence, when he read Tolkien's long novels, he has always viewed his country – especially the wild South Island – through the eyes of fantasy. For him, New Zealand is the mythical Middle Earth. We have to agree. Take Queenstown, for example. Within the radius of at most a two-hour drive from the city one can find the amazing scenery of Lake Wanaka, the snow-capped peaks of the Southern Alps (the mountains that served as 'training grounds' for the New Zealander Sir Edmund Hillary, the first person to conquer Mt. Everest's summit), and the even more astonishing nature of Fiordland National Park. With a surface area of nearly 3 million acres, it boasts mountains as high as 8858 feet, 14 extremely deep fjords, and hundreds upon hundreds of glacial lakes, streams, and forests whose ground is overgrown with equally surreal ferns. The natives of New Zealand, the Maori, call this territory *Ata Whenua* or Shadowland, because the sun only rarely manages to penetrate the thick clouds that cover its valleys. Add to this the fact that the area is home to the *weta*, the heaviest insect (weighing up to 2.5 ounces), the *tuatara* (a lizard and last survivor of the most ancient family of reptiles, the *Sphenodontia*, which became extinct 100 million years ago), and the *kea*, the only mountain parrot. Then there are the sheep – so many that they are a permanent feature of the landscape. Indeed, there are 10 times more sheep than human beings in New Zealand (the population is barely 4 million, very low for a country just a bit larger than Italy).

36 - A marvelous sunset bathing the landscape of Queenstown, the 'world adventure capital,' as New Zealanders call it, on the shores of Lake Wakatipu.

37 - The turquoise water of Lake Wakatipu and the snow-capped peaks of the Southern Alps serve as the backdrop to Matakauri Lodge, an 'out-of-this- world' deluxe oasis where you can relax and take a bath in a Jacuzzi with a panoramic view after one of the thousand adventures offered by Queenstown.

38 - A perfect rainbow created by the spray from the falls that plunge into Milford Sound, in Fiordland National Park.

38 / 39 - Deep fjords – the waters of which are purple thanks to the presence of certain algae – stunning mountains, and forests form the surreal landscape of Fiordland Park, which, quite understandably, was one of the locations for where the *Lord of the Ring* and *Hobbit* fantasy trilogies were shot.

The grandiose nature, the green so intense that it seems to have been photographically retouchec, and the sensation of splendid isolation afforded by the security that you will hardly ever come across another person during a car ride or hike – all this makes the South Island seem like the land of elves and othe᾿ fantastic creatures. All these things impart a dreamlike dimension to these places – and to your vacation. In order to enjoy it to the full, book a romantic suite – with a rigorously contemporary and chic style – at the splendid Matakauri Lodge, immersed in a solitary 'end of the world' settings only 7 minutes by car from Queenstown – just in case you miss life in a city, albeit a small one.

Bali
Indonesia

Rangda is a witch, a female demon depicted with a long, menacing tongue and bristly, bright yellow hair. Barong, on the other hand, is a priest who in order to combat Rangda takes on the appearance of a dragon. In the Balinese epic these two characters represent Evil and Good, and their struggle is staged every evening in the fantastic setting of one of the many, highly decorated temples of Ubud.

The play is endless and very hard to follow, but the 'theater' is always full of enthusiastic tourists who try to grasp the spirit of Bali. In fact, at the root of the fame enjoyed by this island – by far the most popular in the entire and immense Indonesian archipelago, which consists of 17,508 islands – is its culture, which was 'discovered' in the 1930s by artists and anthropologists such as the German Walter Spies, who painted the elegant dancers and serene settings on dream-like canvases, and the American anthropologist Margaret Mead, who in her book, *Balinese Character*, contributed to the creation of the myth of 'magical Bali.' And Ubud, the artists' village in the middle of the island that

became a sort of tropical Montmartre, is the place that made it famous long before people began speaking about its beaches. It is here that today's anthropologists, instead of investigating the customs of the natives, have found it more interesting to study the Westerners who have come on vacation, then settled more or less permanently, thus developing a new field of research termed the anthropology of tourism.

What is so special about Bali is immediately clear: dominated to the north by the tall Gunung Alung volcano, the island has lovely hilly landscapes with rice paddies and coconut palm terraces that share the land with tiny plots of virgin forest. Part of a nation that is the most populated Islamic state in the world, the inhabitants of Bali are followers of a particular form of Hinduism that includes Buddhist features. It goes without saying, therefore, that the island is interspersed with magnificent temples. In terms of architecture and atmosphere, these temples are almost indistinguishable from the resorts, each of which has the inevitable spa and an infinity pool facing a fragrant garden of

40 - At sunset (which should be viewed from the sea) Bali becomes a treasure trove of exoticism and magic.

41 - The Temple of Tanah Lot is one of Bali's chief cons. Built in the 16th century in honor of the sea god, it lies on an islet forged by ocean tides, close to the island's west coast. Local mythology has it that the temple was protected from evil spirits by a gigantic sea serpent.

orchids, frangipani, and ginger flowers. Again, they all have that something extra, which, in its combination of ancient local traditions and contemporary luxury, is the epitome of the Bali style imitated by hotels all over the world. Bali is also special because it doesn't need the classical marriage of white beaches and crystal clear sea that is the *sine qua non* of its competitors. Here the beaches have black volcaric sand, most of which face an ocean with raging waves and strong currents, ideal conditions for mad surfers but quite fatiguing for the 'average' tourist. What's more, when all is said and done the sea in Bali should be admired in ecstatic contemplation – from the cliff of Ulu Watu, or on a walk along the beaches of Kuta, Seminyak and the peninsula of Nusa Dua. But it's better to think twice before taking a dive here. And it's best to think even more before choosing the special resort for your dream vacation in Bali. It is not a question of stars, since all the resorts here have the *Bali style*. What counts is the location. Those seeking a spiritual atmosphere will go to Ubud (and possibly never see the sea), while those looking for beach life will head for Seminyak, which is very, very trendy. For those interested in an intimate nook for a vacation for two, the best option is the astounding Alila Villas Scori, which with its series of villas (each with its own private pool) has elevated the concept of romance and relaxation to the level of Kant.

42 - Surrounded by pools of lotus flowers, the Temple of Pura Taman Saraswati, also known as the Royal Palace on Water, is one of the treasures of Ubud in the heart of the island.

43 *top* - An impressive aerial view of the reef bordering the peninsula of Bukit at the southern end of Bali. Still wild (but not for long, as a group of luxury resorts is soon to be constructed here), Bukit is popular among youth, who go there to vie with the waves on their surfboards.

43 *bottom* - The marvelous Alila Villas Soori are a group of residences with a private pool and a stunning view.

Kyoto
Japan

44 *top* - Gleaming in the sunlight is Kinkaku-ji, the Temple of the Golden Pavilion, one of the most famous in Kyoto. Surrounded by a wonderful garden, it seems to float on the lake.

44 *bottom* - The Hiiragiya ryokan is situated not far from Gion, the most exclusive geisha district in Japan.

45 - Access to the shrine of Fushimi Inari is afforded by a path lined with an extraordinary series of *torii*, traditional Shinto gates.

"The light that filters through the white paper walls, so helpless in its attempt to penetrate the utter darkness of the alcove... creates a world in which light and darkness are indistinguishable, thus imparting a sense of tranquility that one rarely finds elsewhere." This was written by Junichiro Tanizaki, an author whose oeuvre is considered a classic of 20th-century Japanese literature, on one of his frequent visits to Hiiragiya, the *ryokan*, which – founded in 1818 and hidden in a quiet street near the Kyoto Imperial – is one of the most famous traditional inns in the Land of the Rising Sun. Spending a night on the tatami mat in one of the rooms in this (as well as so many other) *ryokan* in Kyoto, after a royal *kaiseki* feast, is a simply priceless aesthetic and cultural experience. What's important is that you not be intimidated by the rigorous ceremony and stubbornly try to understand everything that is taking place around you. Because even more than other famous places in Japan, Kyoto – the nation's capital from 794 to 1868 – embodies the mysteries of this country, where the past and the present (which is dangerously near the future) coexist in a harmonious relationship that is only apparently impossible.

You can get to Kyoto via the high-speed *Shikansen* rail line, which travels so quickly that you practically feel as though you are being teleported. Once there, you can try out the philosophical practice of contemplation, literally enraptured by the rigor and poetry of the city's temples, especially the Kinkaku-ji, the Temple of the Golden Pavilion, which seems to float on the waters of a small lake, and the Ryoan-ji, home to the most famous Zen garden in Japan. And while downtown Kyoto echoes the deafening chaos of the video games created by Nintendo, the hi-tech colossus whose headquarters lie in the heart of Kyoto, you need only cross a bridge to enter the captivating old Gion geisha district, where you may come across these delightful women, so beautiful and refined in their kimonos, as they walk along the cobblestone alleyways. Although Kyoto is a metropolis with 1.5 million busy inhabitants (as we all know, Japan is the country of workaholics), you need only go a few miles out of town to experience the serenity of a rural world at such sites as the mountain shrine of Fushimi Inari, which can be reached by a path with an infinite series of *torii*, traditional Shinto gates painted a dark red. Or you can go to the splendid town of Ohara, which boasts a number of small temples and monasteries amid an extraordinary landscape of maple trees, whose leaves make for an amazing spectacle of color in autumn, and cherry trees, whose wind-swept blossoms blanket the ground in spring. For Japanese culture, such seasonal sights are supreme symbols of the transience of life in this world. And for this very reason they – along with love – should be enjoyed to the full during their magical, unique and ephemeral appearance.

Hangzhou
China

'The Hill of Precious Stones That Floats in a Pink Cloud,' 'The Celestial Wind on Wuhan Hill,' the 'Tiger's Dream in Wupao Valley;' these are only three of the names – taken from the verses of famous Song, Ming and Qing dynasty poets – assigned to the innumerable picturesque settings at West Lake in Hangzhou. According to legend, this body of water with a perimeter of barely 7.4 miles, was created by virtue of a pearl that fell from the sky and became an extraordinary jewel, a lake so beautiful that no other place in China can compete with its evocative power and romantic aura. And though one must have an Eastern mindset to grasp the philosophical aesthetics of Confucian, Buddhist and Taoist cultures, it is also true that Marco Polo, the first Westerner who journeyed here, was spellbound by what he saw and experienced. In his *Travels* he describes Hangzhou as the most sophisticated

city in the world, one that was famous at the time for the manufacturing of silk and cultivation of Longjin or Dragon Well Tea, the most highly prized Chinese green tea.

Agreed, with over 3 million inhabitants and so many manufacturing and hi-tech industries, what is now the capital of Zhejiang Province has changed quite a bit since that time, many centuries ago, when it was one of the seven capitals of the Middle Kingdom. But its high-rise skyline helps remind us of the hordes of visitors (most of them on their honeymoons) that West Lake is not only the "stuff that dreams are made of." It is easy to lose all sense of time while spending the day along its banks, pedaling on a bicycle among bamboo forests or admiring the sunset – splendid all year long – over the water while on a typical local rowboat, or when visiting the temples, caves and pavilions built by

46 - The wonderful pool at the Fuchun Resort, whose glass walls overlook a dreamlike setting of countryside and villages.

47 - Dotted with temples and pavilions that seem to emerge from the water and invite you to linger in ecstatic contemplation of the sunset, West Lake is considered the most romantic and evocative vacation destination in China.

noblemen and emperors with the sole aim of contemplating the beautiful scenery, as in the setting of the Six Harmonies Pagoda, made even more compelling by the 'soundtrack' of 104 bells – one on each of the 8 corners of its 13 floors – that swing in the wind.

West Lake is bordered on one side by the splendid Fuchun Mountains, depicted in a great pen-and-ink painting by the most highly respected Chinese artist of all time, Huang Gongwang (1269-1354). This work – a hand scroll nearly 30 feet long entitled *Dwelling in the Fuchun Mountains* – was damaged by fire in the 17th century and consequently survives in two parts today, one preserved in the Zhejiang Provincial Museum in Hangzhou and the other, larger one, in the National Museum of Taipei.

A tribute to this masterpiece, the captivating Fuchun Resort was built amid the greenery of a dreamlike rural landscape. Designed as a series of pavilions with pagoda roofs, it offers guests the experience of participating in a tea ceremony and enjoying cuisine prepared according to imperial recipes. And, like the painting, it celebrates the harmony between man and nature.

Yunnan Province

China

With 26 ethnic minorities, Yunnan is the most multicultural province in China. In the Imperial Age its inhabitants were considered "the barbarians south of the Yangtze," and were persecuted during the recent Cultural Revolution. Today, however, their customs and traditions are finally being appreciated, and the present-day members of the Communist Party consider the area the cradle of Chinese civilization.

Be that as it may, Yunnan now attracts 30 million Chinese tourists (and barely 450,000 foreigners) each year and is the country's favorite honeymoon destination. In other words, it is to China what Provence is to France and Tuscany to Italy, with the 'subtle' difference that the province is as large as Germany and its landscape ranges from Himalayan highlands to tropical forests. If Kunming, known as 'the city of eternal spring,' is the gate to this province, its heart lies in Lijiang, a town 7874 feet above sea level that consists of an enchanting complex of pagoda-houses, temples, canals, and 365 bridges.

Founded 800 years ago, it was a major marketplace along the 'Tea Road' that crossed over Tibet to connect India and South China. Although an earthquake devastated Lijiang in 1996, the Old Town was rebuilt in record time and is now on the UNESCO World Heritage List. A memento of the past, Lijiang is illuminated in the evening by romantic red lanterns. Its intriguing tearooms serve the highly prized Lu Tie Bing, a black tea of the Pu'er variety that is left to ferment for 35 years before being packaged. In Lijiang you must absolutely visit the Guanyin temple and Black Dragon Pool pagodas, which lie in a location that combines architecture and a bucolic landscape – a triumph of Chinese aesthetics.

Another must is a stay at one of the most romantic resorts in China, the Banyan Tree Lijiang, not far from town. Built in a highly imaginative Ming Dynasty style, its stone and teak-wood pagoda-pavilions house marvelous rooms (all with an outdoor pool that also serves as a Jacuzzi) and a garden affording a panoramic view of *Yulongxue Shan*, or the Jade Dragon Snow Mountain, 18,373 feet high. The slopes of this mountain are a

48 / 49 - Pagodas and a romantic marble bridge are reflected in Black Dragon Pool, one of the most picturesque sights in the town of Lijiang. On clear days you can enjoy the views of Yulongxue Shan or Jade Dragon Snow Mountain, which appear as if by magic in the background of the serene landscape of the Elephant Hill, distinguished by their terraced rice paddies.

50 - The splendid town of Lijiang, once a major stopover along the Tea Road caravan route, is inhabited mostly by members of the Naxi (or Nakhi) people, whose culture is very interesting from an anthropological standpoint.

51 *top* - Situated 6562 feet above sea level in an extremely beautiful natural setting, the Banyan Tree Resort was modeled after Ming Dynasty architecture.

51 *bottom* - The BaiYun restaurant at the Banyan Tree Lijiang Resort offers excellent Cantonese nouvelle cuisine in an elegant pavilion bordered by greenery and a pool with koi carp, the fish that according to Chinese tradition is the symbol of good luck and prosperity.

favorite with hikers who visit the villages of the Naxi, a fascinating ethnic group from an anthropological standpoint known for its rich traditional clothing and *dongba* script, the only one in the world still based on pictograms. Beyond Lijiang, and rivaling it as a romantic site, is Dali City, where you can visit the famous Three Pagodas, built in the 12th century and considered one of the most important Buddhist monuments in China. Among the many natural sights in Yunnan certainly the most extraordinary are Tiger Leaping Gorge, the deepest in the world, and Shilin or Stone Forest. Likewise included in the UNESCO World Heritage List, the latter is a stretch of limestone pinnacles formed by 270 million years of erosion and rising up from the vegetation and thus creating a surreal impression of a perennial garden. Chinese couples have themselves photographed there as a token of their eternal love.

In the Valleys of Bhutan
Bhutan

At the marvelous Taktshang Goempa (Tiger's Nest) Buddhist monastery, suspended on a rocky spur at an altitude of 10,236 feet in the Paro Valley, you will certainly meet a monk who will explain to you – as if it were an incontrovertible fact – that the site was founded by the Guru Rimpoche, who arrived by flying on a winged tiger from Tibet. What is astonishing is that you will find this story absolutely convincing…

After all, even the flight you took from Delhi or Kathmandu – looking down over a region with 9 of the 14 tallest peaks in the world – to this remote Himalayan kingdom was a magical experience. Once you landed at Paro, you found yourself in another world, one that undermined all the rules to which you have been accustomed. It may seem incredible – yet it is has been proven – but in this era of global economy, Bhutan is prospering in splendid isolation. Here, according to a decree issued by the beloved sovereign, His Majesty Druk Gyalpo Jigme Dorji Wangchuck III, the wealth of the country is measured not by GDP but by GDH (Gross Domestic Happiness), which is calculated on the basis of four basic criteria: the righteous well-being of the king's 6000 subjects, respect for the environment, protection of the country's spiritual and cultural heritage, and good government. In short, this kingdom, covering an area of 18,147 square miles that lie 6562 to 22,966 feet above sea level, is the transposition of the legendary Shangri-La, where beatitude can be experienced through a pilgrimage that is both geographical and spiritual.

It goes without saying that the starting point for any itinerary, among enchanting valleys, rhododendron forests and centuries-old monasteries, is the Paro Valley, where you can stay at the romantic Uma by Como resort, immersed in beautiful scenery and featuring luxury suites and spas where you can 'recharge' after the fatigue of the journey through Asian inspired treatment. And for honeymooners this high-class hotel organizes a Buddhist blessing ceremony to invoke a happy marriage; it is officiated by the Lama of the Taktshang monastery in the dim, dream-like light of yak butter lamps.

52 - Made of stone and wood, and with a handmade terracotta tile roof, the villas of the Uma by Como resort are a (luxurious) tribute to Himalayan Buddhist culture. They are in the middle of the mystical forest in the Paro Valley, the flora of which is dominated by rhododendrons, azaleas and hydrangeas.

53 - Something one should not miss while in the Himalayan kingdom of Bhutan is a trek along this difficult path to Taktshang Goempa.

Hoi An

Vietnam

54 - At Hoi An the fishermen still follow use traditional methods, casting nets as they navigate the Thu Bon River estuary or the open sea in their curiously rounded boats.

55 - In the evening, when the lanterns are lit, a truly romantic atmosphere overtakes the riverbanks of Hoi An, that reminding us of one of those scenes in Marguerite Duras's novel, *The Lover*. Now a UNESCO World Heritage Site, the town is an exceptional example of a well-preserved Southeast Asian commercial port.

On the 15th night of each month of the lunar calendar, all electric lights are turned off in Hoi An as the city becomes illuminated by a phantasmagoria of ethereal lanterns made of colored silk, which are the pride and joy of local craftsmen. The shops here gleam with assorted lacquers, jade, ceramics and silk embroidery that are as lovely as paintings. Tourists stand in line in small restaurants to taste the *cao lau* noodles, which seem to owe their exquisite taste to the fact that they are kneaded with water from an ancient well situated near the marketplace. Tailors' and dressmakers' workshops – there are 200 here, another source of local flame – resound with the whirr of old pedaled Singer sewing machines, a noise that merges with notes from the Chinese Opera performed on a stage set up along the riverside and the clanging of bicycles and *cyclos* or mopeds, the only means of transportation permitted in the old town. It's like being in a movie, or better, in one of the many films shot in this area, from *Indochine* starring an unforgettable Catherine Deneuve to *The Lover*, a cinematic version of the passionate love affair narrated in Marguerite Duras' novel of the same name.

Protected by UNESCO as one of the sites on the World Heritage List, Hoi An is the most romantic place in Vietnam, perfect for a few days' break during a tour of the country. Situated on the estuary of the Thu Bon River halfway between Hanoi and Ho Chi Minh City, the metropolises of the North and South respectively, and a comfortable distance from the equally splendid city of Hué, the ancient capital of the Vietnamese kingdom during the Nguyen dynasty, Hoi An was for many centuries the main trading harbor in the South China Sea. Here, from the 16th century on, local merchants flanked by their Japanese confrères built their own enclave, separated from the local one by a lovely bridge that is now one of the most photographed monuments in the historic center and which still supports an exceptional group of houses. The latter – occupied but open to visitors – were built from the 17th to the 19th century and are decorated with Oriental furniture and *objets d'art*, thus offering tourists a glimpse of a lifestyle that is still deeply rooted in ancient traditions, the most important of which is ancestor worship.

The atmosphere of Hoi An should be absorbed slowly. It is worth one's while to rent a bicycle to ride on perfectly straight paths that cross peaceful green rice paddies and coconut tree groves, leading all the way to the sea. Here, in one section of the beautiful and endless Cua Dai beach, lies the most stylish and luxurious resort in the country, The Nam Hai, the architecture of which was modeled after the royal residences in Hué. The Nam Hai offers guests a gamut of cultural experiences, including visits to handicrafts workshops, lessons in Vietnamese cuisine, and shellfish fishing with expert local fishermen.

56 - The coastline between Hoi An and Da Nang consists of a series of splendid beaches facing the South China Sea. About 6 miles from Hoi An, picturesque Ha My Beach boasts the luxurious The Nam Hai resort, situated in a palm grove.

57 - The Nam Hai resort pampers its guests with romantic aperitifs in an elegant lounging area out on the beach. One of the most exclusive resorts in Vietnam, its chic contemporary architecture is modeled after that of the royal city of Hué.

Luang Prabang
Laos

Every morning at exactly 6 o'clock the monks, each carrying a metal bowl, leave the temples in single file and slowly walk along the streets of Luang Prabang. All the inhabitants wait for the monks at the front doors of their homes and give them sticky rice and vegetables as alms, thus performing the Tak Bat ritual, which dates back to the oldest of the Buddhist temples. For the faithful alms-giver, a monk's acceptance of alms is tantamount to a benediction of the donor, who thus acquires a merit for his or her future reincarnation. For tourists, on the other hand, watching this ceremony is a unique opportunity to comprehend the culture of the ancient capital of Laos, the most traditionalist country in Southeast Asia, and still deeply rooted in Buddhist spiritual practice.

Certainly in the rarefied atmosphere just after dawn, when the morning mist rising from the Mekong River envelopes the buildings of Luang Prabang in a sort of bridal veil, the image of the long, winding row of Buddhist monks in their saffron robes is an invitation to take photos. But one must be careful because this is not a

show but a religious ceremony. In fact, Buddhist authorities and the municipal administration have published a brochure listing regulations for tourists: they must remain silent, wear modest clothing (with shoulders, legs and torsos covered), and be seated without exposing the soles of their feet as the procession passes.

This is a question of respect; just as we must respect every square foot of this city, which boasts 35 magnificent temples – all immersed in a serene, scented tropical setting – mostly of teak wood with intricate low-reliefs, gilding and mirrors, as well as hundreds – sometimes thousands – of Buddha statues of every size.

Respect for the local culture is a hallmark of the numerous and highly fascinating hotels of Luang Prabang, many of which belong to families related to the ancient royal house, or are aristocratic mansions and estates converted into luxury lodgings. Among these, the most romantic is Belmond La Résidence Phou Vao, which, besides offering top-quality hospitality, offers many activities to its guests: visits to nearby country villages, an excursion on traditional

58 - Thirty-three feet high and covered with gold leaf, the statue of the so-called Giant Buddha dominates the Mekong River from a hill, on a level with the town of Pakse, in southern Laos.

59 - A very young monk at the entrance to Wat Manolom. Although this is neither the oldest nor most elaborate temple here, it demands a visit as it houses the largest monastic community and most important school for novices in Luang Prabang.

60 - Hidden in a peaceful forest setting about 18 miles from Luang Prabang, Kuang Si Falls create many idyllic natural pools. During the hot season swimming here is a necessary ritual.

61 *top* - The intimate suites at Belmond La Résidence Phou Vao overlook a pool dotted with white water lilies and lotuses.

61 *bottom* - Surrounded by a luxuriant tropical garden and lying on a hill a short distance from Luang Prabang, is the exceptional Belmond La Résidence Phou Vao, which boasts wonderful architecture and a dreamlike atmosphere redolent of the French colonial period.

vessels along the Mekong River to see the famous holy caves of Pak Ou (which hold 10,000 statues of Buddha), and courses in local cuisine, including lessons in preparing sticky rice, the mainstay of the Laotian diet. Couples can also undergo the Baci, an auspicious ceremony officiated by a shaman with the alleged power to make relationships more harmonious and solid.

Indeed, the sense of harmony is what remains in your heart after a stay at Luang Prabang, with its thousand years of history, infinitely serene landscape, and inhabitants who are among the most tenderhearted in Asia. Here it is a pleasure to exchange small gifts of love purchased at the colorful market or to enjoy moments of sheer beatitude by nearby Kuang waterfalls, which, hidden in the forest, form a series of natural pools of a brilliant turquoise color. A swim here too is 'almost' a sacred ritual.

Angkor
Cambodia

62 - Known as the 'Mona Lisas of Southeast Asia,' the gigantic and enigmatic faces of the bodhisattva Avalokiteshvara sculpted onto the Temple of Bayon are among the most intriguing marvels of the ancient Khmer capital of Angkor. The city's architecture served as a model for the pavilions that surround the pool of the Raffles Grand Hotel d'Angkor, which opened in 1932 and still preserves its colonial charm.

63 - An aerial view of the magnificent Angkor Wat, which, with a perimeter of 2.5 miles, is the largest religious monument in the world.

You must get up very early in the morning to arrive in Angkor before hordes of visitors upset the peace and quiet of the forest. Go first to the Ta Phrom temple and sit for a while on a stone in one of the courtyards to contemplate the ruins, which are caught in the grip of vegetation that has invaded and overrun the stones over the centuries. The roots of the trees make their way among the blocks until emerging from the ruins, they extend their arms, embrace the columns, and cling to window ornaments. In the penumbra created by the branches and foliage, nature and human architecture become a single living being. The Ta Phrom temple is by no means the most majestic or exquisite work produced by the Khmer Empire. But it captures the atmosphere that must have greeted the French traveler Henri Mouhot in 1858, the date that marks European discovery of Angkor. This is what all temples must have looked like before archeologists sent to the French colony of Indochina disentangled this exceptional city from the forest to reveal to the world the remains of the most refined civilization in Southeast Asia. You need at least three days to visit Angkor, experience its magic and let yourself be transported by the stories depicted in the miles of bas-relief that decorate the perimeter and corridors of Angkor Wat, the grandiose temple mountain that is the greatest achievement of the Khmer civilization. At sunset you can watch the elegant young Cambodian women, who each day perform the movements of the *apsara*, the celestial dancers of Buddhist tradition, right before the monument. Then you must take the

time to contemplate the gigantic, enigmatic sculpted faces of the Bayon temple in the middle of Angkor Thom, the citadel and last capital of Khmer power. Or again, go visit Banteay Srei, the "citadel of women," so admirably described in *The Royal Way*, the autobiographical 1930 novel by French author André Malraux and still a fascinating evocative guidebook to the gems of Cambodia. In Angkor you actually lose perception of time, even when, beyond the archeological zone, you wander off to the floating villages of Torle Sap or Great Lake, a kind of liquid highway between this spectacular site and Phnom Penh, the chaotic and mysterious capital of Cambodia. Even Siem Reap, a village just outside Angkor that has grown uncontrollably into a lively modern tourist city, has sights that go back to the time the temples were discovered.

Among these, mention must be made of the Raffles Grand Hotel d'Angkor, which opened in 1932 and still preserves a sophisticated colonial atmosphere full of luxurious furnishings and marvelous details. Doormen's trousers! The uniform is inspired by costumes found in the Royal family's court treasure chest. There are different colored trousers for each day of the week, which is believed to bring good luck. The King will observe and know exactly what day of the week it is! Monday – Orange / Tuesday – Dark purple / Wednesday – Light green / Thursday – Green / Friday – Royal Blue / Saturday – Plum / Sunday – Red. The tradition continues today at Raffles Grand Hotel d'Angkor: first and foremost a highly romantic candlelight dinner by the water's edge while facing Angkor War.

Krabi
Thailand

64 - The guests at the Rayavadee Resort at Krabi stay in luxurious suites (called pavilions here) surrounded by tropical vegetation and a private pool.

65 - These absolutely vertical granite cliffs, which rise from the beach and are ideal for free climbing, a forest, coconut orchards and, above all, twin bays with white sand skirt the Andaman (or Burma) Sea. These are the marvels of the Phranang peninsula, one of the most popular destinations in southern Thailand, a truly splendid area, most of which is preserved as a national park.

"Same same but different" is the phrase that the Thai repeat like a mantra in all their conversation, from comments on the beauty of a beach to the quality of a souvenir. And though, as far as physical features go – transparent seas, white sands, palm trees caressed by a breeze – all the coastlines and islands of the Adaman Sea can be deemed roughly identical, those in Thailand are different because they belong to the Thai people, who have elevated the art of hospitality to the level of the sublime. Courtesy is part and parcel of their character and genes and is clearly visible in their delicate facial features, always ready to brighten up with a disarming smile – so much so that here the *farang* (their term for foreigners) feel spoiled as in no other place on earth. You will realize this as soon as you receive the gift that welcomes all visitors when they arrive at a resort, a garland of orchids and jasmine with an intoxicating fragrance, a perfect harbinger of the sublime pleasure that awaits them during their vacation.

This said, we must admit that it was more difficult in this case than in any other destination described in this book to choose the resort most suitable for a couple in love. From the renowned Phuket to the equally famous Ko Phi Phi, or – if we take into consideration more out-of-the-way islands, such as Ko Lanta with its picturesque villages built on stilts and known as *Moken*, 'gypsies of the sea,' – the number of dream destinations is virtually infinite. After a great deal of thought, however, we decided to recommend the Rayavadee because surveys conducted by leading travel periodicals have rated

it one of the world's best hotels. The reason lies in its unique position on the tip of the peninsula of Phranang, in the heart of an extensive network of marine and land reserves in the province of Krabi. Another reason lies in the fact that the road on the way to the garland ritual runs past majestic rock pinnacles and coconut palm plantations, creating the feeling of a secret, enchanted world. A bit like what happens to the protagonists of the novel (and movie) *The Beach*.

It seems almost superfluous to add that the architecture of the Rayavadee resort is highly luxurious style (rooms are known as pavilions), that the cuisine will stimulate your senses, and that the spa is one of the most prestigious in Thailand, a country famous for massage. What is truly crucial, however, is that once there you are within striking distance of all the most extraordinary sights in southern Thailand, from the above-mentioned Ko Phi Phi to the Ao Phang-Nga National Park, an exceptional 'forest' of rock formations that emerges from the sea, and the cliffs looming over Railay Bay, which offer rock climbing for the adventurous. And, located a little further south of the Rayavadee, is the islet of Ko Kradan, in the Ko Lanta archipelago, the venue of what is listed in the Guinness Book of World Records as the largest collective underwater wedding in the world, which takes place on Valentine's Day. Officiated according to a Buddhist rite, it is accompanied by a Thai-style feast on the beach. The ceremony is not legally binding, but the event is one of those that will remain in your heart for the rest of your life.

Chiang Mai
Thailand

66 *top* - Not far from Chiang Rai, in the heart of the Golden Triangle, is Wat Rong Khun, a phantasmagorical white temple that combines Buddhist tradition and New Age architecture, and was designed by the imaginative artist Chalermchai Kositpipat.

66 *bottom* - The majestic lobby to the Dhara Dhevi luxury resort, modeled after the imperial palace of the Lanna, the ancient rulers of Chiang Mai.

67 - Doi Inthanon National Park, with its splendid royal pagodas.

For many centuries Chiang Mai was the capital of the Lanna Kingdom, which, at its peak, dominated northern Thailand, Burma, Laos and southern China. At present, however, the city must content itself (so to speak) with its status as the heart of the Golden Triangle, one of the main attractions of Thailand, which, more than any other country in Asia, has transformed itself into a dream factory for tourists interested in exotic adventures that offer comfort and luxury. Here everything is possible, you can spend your day in a state of pleasant elation with a visit to one of the temples, a lesson in spicy Thai cuisine, a tour of the botanical gardens – where you can discover the existence of languid orchids with the sweet scent of chocolate – or of an elephant sanctuary, where you can watch these creatures take their daily bath in the river. From Chiang Mai you can go for a hike in mountains carpeted with a thick forest or try your hand at rafting on a rudimentary bamboo raft. Afterwards you spend the night in a rented house on stilts in one of the Golden Triangle villages populated by the many ethnic minorities. At Chiang Mai you can go shopping until late at night, browsing among the hundreds of colorful handicraft objects at the marvelous Night Market. And should you be here during the 12th full moon according to the traditional local lunar calendar – in late October or November – you can experience the magic of the Loi Khrathong light festival, during which thousands of

persons gather on the banks of the Ping River to honor Buddha, as did the ancient subjects of the Kingdom of Lanna, place offerings made of banana leaves and flowers in the water, and toss myriads of paper lanterns filled with hot air into the air in a spectacle that will be a delight for photography buffs. In sum, Chiang Mai is a fabulous destination that should be enjoyed to the full by booking a colonial suite at the luxurious Dhara Dhevi, a resort modeled on the Lanna imperial palace. Situated in a 30-hectare area, this is a true fantasyland of teak wood constructions, majestic gilt temples with multicolored mirrors, massive fortifications, tropical gardens, central cerimonial lawn, streams, huge swimming pools, and even a market and a rice plantation cultivated by 'old-fashioned farmers' with the help of wooden plows drawn by water buffaloes. The alpha and omega of the complex is the prayer hall, a perfect replica of the Wat Prathat Lampang Luang temple that serves as the symbol of Lanna power and lies about 50 miles from Chiang Mai, and the Dheva Spa, a palace of well-being and of Oriental philosophy topped by a stupa that symbolizes the path of purification towards nirvana. A state you may attain, by the way, in a purely 'secular' manner through an invigorating tok sen massage, which is performed with a small tamarind wood hammer in keeping with a 15th-century ritual performed at the Lanna court.

68 - The fantastic pool in the Colonial Wing of the Dhara Dhevi resort. One hundred and fifty master craftsmen from this capital city of the North worked more than three years on the decoration of the Dheva Spa and Wellness Center.

69 *top* - The resort's Penthouse Residence is equipped with sumptuous colonial furniture and Persian carpets. Even a grand piano.

69 *bottom* - With an aura of grandeur reminiscent of the ancient palace, the Royal Residence at the Dhara Dhevi resort has a series of pavilions surrounded by fragrant gardens that offer the very best in luxury and intimacy.

Along the Irrawaddy
Myanmar

The beauty secret of Burmese women is called thanakha. This is the yellowish paste obtained from the bark of a tree, the *Limonia acidissima* or wood-apple, which has a faint sandalwood aroma. For over 2000 years it has protected people's skin from the sun, made it more elastic and relaxed, and been used as a fantastic blush for the cheeks. In fact, in Burma (or Myanmar, now the country's official name) there is still no market for modern cosmetics. Few men and women wear Western clothing and the *de rigueur* attire is the *longyi*, a local version of the sarong. Furthermore, you won't be able to find an automated teller machine in the entire country and will go crazy trying to locate decent Internet access.

More than a century ago, the author Rudyard Kipling – who was well acquainted with India and its customs – described Burma as a place completely different from any other. This still holds true today even though the country has finally made contact with the outside world after decades of brutal military dictatorship and today offers visitors romantic echoes of what it was like during British colonial rule.

While by now the skyline of all Asian metropolises is dominated by a forest of high-rises, the hub of Yangon, the only large city in Burma, is the golden mountain – visible from any viewpoint – of the Shwedagon Pagoda, which is 2600 years old and holds the record as the oldest pagoda in the world. A visit to this sacred monument, which is always filled with monks in saffron robes and pilgrims, is an absolute must before penetrating into the labyrinth of this fascinating city – comprised of multicolored markets and spectral, Neo-Gothic colonial buildings – the starting point of any itinerary in this country. Among the many possible trips, the most adventurous lead to the mountains, where interesting ethnic minorities reside, or to the coastlines and unspoiled islands of the Andaman (or Burma) Sea. But the most dream-like and seductive of all is the trip along the Irrawaddy, Burma's longest river, on one of the two ships that Belmond company reserves for refined and cultured tourists. The vessel moves slowly in order to allow passengers to enjoy the countryside along the banks, including views of

70 / 71 - The luxury ship that navigates along the Irrawaddy River is called the *Belmond Road to Mandalay*. Along this river's banks lie the treasures of Burma, the most precious of which is Bagan, which boasts 10,000 magnificent temples.

village life. The tour proceeds up to Bagan, one of the most impressive religious and cultural sites on the continent, with around 10,000 Buddhist temples and stupas (each of which is unique) that emerge from an amazing setting of palm trees and sacred banyan trees. Bagan should be explored on foot or horse-drawn carriage, as in Kipling's time. The site becomes a true dream at sunset. There is plenty of time to enjoy and meditate on this spectacle before heading to the capital of the ancient Kingdom of Burma, Mandalay, a gem on the bend of a river. Awaiting you here is a royal palace complex of numerous teak wood buildings as well as another series of magnificent temples, each of which has its own community of monks and their women, who, with their cheeks highlighted with *thanakha*, spend the day making garlands of flowers for Buddha.

Agra

India

According to a custom in the Moghul court, women replaced merchants at the Agra bazaar once a year to pretend to sell silk and jewels. It was on this occasion, in 1607, that the two met. The man, who later became the Shah Jahan, the 'king of the world,' and under whose rule the empire attained its apogee, was 17 at the time. She, Ariumand Bano Begum, the daughter of a Persian dignitary, was 16. They married a short time afterwards. Although the Shah had other wives and a harem of no fewer than 5000 concubines, she was always Mumtaz Mahal, the 'palace favorite.' When – 24 years and 14 children later – she died during childbirth, the emperor decided to construct a magnificent tomb that would celebrate their love forever.

This, in short, is the story of the Taj Mahal, which the British author Rudyard Kipling called "the Ivory Gate through which all good dreams come." There is no monument as romantic as this in all of India, and perhaps in the entire world. It took 20,000 laborers, artisans and artists (who lived in Taj Ganj, the quarter built for them that is now the

heart of Agra) 20 years to build, on the banks of the Jamuna River, this white marble jewel topped by a huge dome 246 feet high and framed by four tall minarets at the structure's cardinal points. This 'poem in stone' is adorned with a forest of stone-hewn flowers that impart an ethereal grace and lightness to the complex.

To take in all its enchanting beauty you must proceed step by step, by first booking a room at The Oberoi Amarvilas, Agra, one of the most exclusive hotels in India, whose architecture, decor and atmosphere evoke the splendor of the Moghul period. The hotel provides a perfect view of the monument situated only 722 yards away. As you look at it early in the morning from your window when the first rays of sunlight paint it pink and the fog rises from the waters of the Jamuna River, the Taj Mahal seems nearly suspended in empty space – a truly dream-like experience, and, it should be added, the best way to prepare for your visit to this masterpiece. Populated by the descendants of the artists and artisans who made it, Agra has other marvelous monuments in store.

72 / 73 - The splendid arcade of the Diwan-i-Am, used by the Moghul rulers as a hall of public audience, is one of the remarkable attractions at the Red Fort. The center of imperial power, the fort lies a mile or so from the Taj Mahal, the most famous monument in Agra, and indeed in all of India. This fabulous tribute to eternal love was poetically described by Rudyard Kipling as "the Ivory Gate through which all good dreams come."

First among these is the Red Fort, the royal residence that served as the seat of the empire and setting for Shah Jahan and Mumtaz Mahal's love story.

A short distance from the city, a journey into the history of Moghul architecture must include Fatehpur Sikri, the 'ghost city' that served as the empire's capital before Agra with its splendid mosque that is still visited by women of all religions who wish to have children. Finally, 25 miles from Agra, lies Mathura, a major Hindu pilgrimage site because it is the birthplace of Khrishna. The Hindu god of love and joy is celebrated here and in the entire subcontinent in late February-early March with the fantastic, colorful Holi festival.

74 - Fascinating Fatehpur Sikri or City of Victory is situated about 22 miles from Agra. It was built as the capital of his empire in 1571 by the Moghul Emperor Akbar, but was abandoned for reasons unknown 15 years later.

75 *top* - Surrounded by elegant pavilions in perfect Moghul style, the pool of The Oberoi Amarvilas, Agra, one of the most exclusive hotels on the subcontinent, is an invitation to relax after a visit to the Taj Mahal.

75 *bottom* - The most romantic rooms in The Oberoi Amarvilas, Agra, are those with a magnificent panoramic view of the dome and towers of the Taj Mahal.

Jaipur
India

Invited to a dinner by a maharaja during a trip to India, the American millionaire Barbara Hutton decided to show off her black pearl necklace. You can imagine her disappointment when her host, after paying her a compliment for her 'bauble,' proceeded to show her his jewels: a chest full of black pearls and others with diamonds, rubies, and emeralds. For an Indian prince, after all, these were everyday objects... As British author Rudyard Kipling once noted, God had created maharajas so that the world could enjoy the spectacle of their treasures.

Census data have shown that there are 565 princely families in the Indian subcontinent. Officially, of course, their title holds no value nowadays. In addition, many of them, who are no longer as rich as they once were have made a virtue of necessity by opening their fabulous palaces to paying visitors. Among these are the (ex) rulers of Jaipur, the capital of Rajasthan, the so-called State of Princes, where, until her death in 2009, the maharani Gayatri Devi lived in a 'modest' wing of the 19th-century Rambagh Palace, which

she had converted into one of the most romantic and luxurious hotels in the world. In the halls and corridors of what could be your residence for a few nights, lingers the spirit of that exceptional woman who scandalized India by marrying for love, defying convention and reasons of state. In any case, it is impossible not to fall in love in Jaipur, just as it is impossible not to fall in love with Jaipur itself, where the pink city walls and buildings serve as a canvas for the bright colors of women's saris and the spices of the bazaars.

Jaipur is a treasure chest of marvels. It was founded in 1728 by Sawai Jai Singh, the maharaja who ordered the construction of the amazing Jantar Mantar, an observatory with 14 architectural structures used as astronomical 'instruments' for observing the stars and calculating their exact position; the findings were then given to court astrologers for further interpretation. Another marvel is the Hawa Mahal, or Palace of the Winds, whose facade is decorated with 953 small windows protected by delicately carved sandstone latticework that allowed women in the harem to

76 / 77 - The capital of the state of Rajasthan is a trove of architectural treasures. Among these is the façade of the Hawa Mahal, the Palace of the Winds, with latticework that resembles embroidery and 953 small windows from which the women in the harem could look outside without being seen. Another treasure is the complex of pink buildings, formerly the residence of the maharajas of Jaipur, but now a museum housing precious objects.

look outside without being seen. There is also the labyrinthine complex of buildings of the City Palace, which houses a museum of extravagant princely items, including two silver jars each weighing 760 pounds that the maharaja Sawai Madho Singh commissioned to transport the holy water of the Ganges for his ablutions while he was traveling. Again, standing on a hill just outside the center of town is the Amber Fort, once a defensive fortification and site of sensual pleasure. It even has an incredible alcove entirely covered with small mirrors that imitate a magical starry night for the maharaja's use. In order to arrive at this magical structure, do as the princes must have done: for a few rupees, go up the winding paved road that leads to main gate on an elephant decked out in rich trappings.

Actually, the nights at the Rambagh Palace and the elephant ride are only two of the many dream experiences you can enjoy during your vacation here. Another, an essential one, is a visit to the Gem Palace, the most prestigious jeweler in Jaipur, also known as the world capital of gem cutting. Give one mounted on an oriental ring, to your sweetheart and she will remain your maharani forever.

78 - Built in the late 16th century, the fabulous Amber Fort dominates Lake Maota from a hill about 7 miles from Jaipur. Despite being a military structure, it looks like an opulent palace of sensual pleasure.

79 *top* - Situated a short distance from the pink walls of Jaipur is Rambagh Palace, converted into a luxury hotel already in 1957. This marvelous structure was erected in 1835 as the residence of the Infant Prince Ram Singh II and his wet-nurse.

79 *bottom* - In addition to its rich collection of art objects, Rambagh Palace is also known for its outstanding series of pavilions and gardens.

Galle

Sri Lanka

The word 'serendipity' became known in the Western World in the 18th century thanks to the English diplomat and author, Sir Horace Walpole, who used it in a letter to a friend. Walpole drew inspiration from an ancient Persian fable, *The Three Princes of Serendip*, in which the princes make a series of unexpected discoveries thanks to their intuition and great luck. Serendip is a word that Arabs took from the Sanskrit *Simhaladvipa*, or 'Island Where Lions Dwell,' to name the large tear-shaped island now known as Sri Lanka, the 'Resplendent Island.'

Few places in the world can boast such a magnificent variety of landscapes, cultures, biodiversity and, above all, impressions in such a small area, so much so that one expects to make a fortunate discovery at every curve of its inaccessible roads. In short, serendipity is part of Sri Lanka's destiny. The same serendipity that in 1505 caused a Portuguese ship to land here after it had lost its way pursuing a fleet of Arab merchants on their way to the Maldives with a cargo of spices, an accidental event that marked the beginning of

the island's colonial history. Allegedly the sailors heard a rooster crowing from the shore and thus called that promontory *Galo*.

Situated on the southwestern tip of Sri Lanka, in a strategic point along the route from Arabia and Africa to the Far East, is the city known today as Galle, which boasts a large fort placed on the UNESCO World Heritage List as a unique colonial urban ensemble in South Asia. The only trace of the city's domination by the Portuguese is the so-called Black Bastion, the oldest surviving portion of the Santa Cruz Fort. On the other hand, there are innumerable examples of the heritage of the Dutch, who in 1640 wrested the city from the Portuguese and ruled it until 1796, when the British took it over. On the promontory the Dutch built a fort with two large gates – one of which displayed the coat of arms of the Dutch East Indies Company with the abbreviation VOC (United East India Company) carved in stone – as well as impressive churches and buildings. As for the pragmatic English, they limited their activity largely to 'occupying' Dutch structures, which came to serve as the

80 / 81 - Ideal for a long walk at sunset while listening to the music of the palm leaves caressed by the wind, Unawatuna is one of the most beautiful beaches on the coastline of Galle. Here, as in nearby Weligama beach, you can watch the spectacle of a fishermen precariously balanced on stilts driven a few inches into the sand, an old fishing technique still in use among the 500 local families.

administrative center of the colony. They also built elegant residences for the governor and high officials in or just outside the fort, some of which have been converted into colonial style hotels with teak furniture and the ubiquitous portraits of Queen Victoria and Queen Elizabeth II. All of Galle fort, however, is an absolutely romantic destination. Its bazaar, strong scent of spices, and steep paths along cliffs, seem to belong to another time. You need go only a few miles outside of Galle – on the traditional tuk-tuk – to experience the serendipity of the most beautiful beaches of Sri Lanka, from Wijaya to Mirissa and Weligama and Unawatuna, famous for the men who fish while balancing themselves precariously on stilts. But no sooner do you go inland for even a short distance, than you will discover a world of pristine forests, rice paddies and plantations of tea, the island's principal export. Right in the middle of one such organic tea plantation is Kahanda Kanda, a marvelous resort that is truly a discovery. With only 9 suites in a garden populated by parrots and peacocks, it offers relaxation as well as many interesting activities for its guests – from cooking lessons to boat excursions in nearby Koggala Lake, where a family has run a cinnamon plantation on a small island since the time of Portuguese dominion.

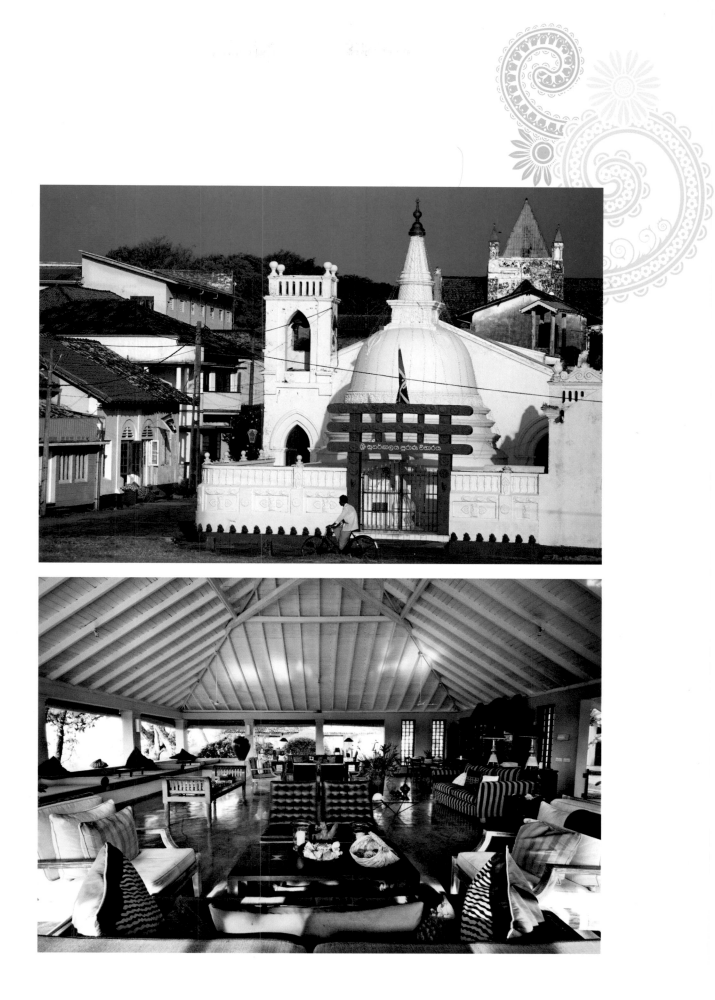

82 - Founded by the Portuguese, Galle was an important possession of the Dutch East Indies Company from 1640 to 1796. From here Dutch ships returned to Europe laden with spices and, above all, tea, which thrives on the fertile hills of the ancient island of Ceylon.

83 - The old fort in Galle is an example of harmonious coexistence as it is inhabited by Tamils of Hindu faith, Muslims, and Singhalese who are equally divided among Christians and Buddhists. A few miles away from this delightful coastal city and situated in the luxuriant interior, is the romantic Kahanda Kanda Resort.

The Maldive Islands

Republic of the Maldives

It goes without saying that the Maldives Tourist Bureau does not need to use spectacular language and images to promote a dream vacation site such as this nation of islands. But the slogan '99% water' – accompanied by a photograph of a couple lying languidly on a tiny strip of white sand surrounded by water of an almost fluorescent turquoise without the aid of Photoshop – might be considered one of the most appropriate though least 'creative' ever conceived because if you calculate the surface area of this republic by setting the border at the outer edge of its 26 atolls, and then subtract the surface area of the 1192 islands, the ratio between sea and land is 99 to 1. In short, a magnificent nothing. At this point you might object that it is easy enough to say 'nothing,' but beneath that 99% of water lies an entire world (one of the most spectacular on our planet, by the way) of marine life, including corals and fish of every color and size. And you might add that one could quite easily lie for hours on end in utter idleness, and with great pleasure, in these calm, warm waters with their extraordinarily subtle color nuances. As for the tiny part that lies above the surface, you need nothing more for a vacation than an enchanting beach and the shade of coconut palms. Naturally, there are also those 21st-century Robinson Crusoe delights represented by the multitude of resorts that dot the archipelago, each on its own exclusive island, which is often so small that it takes no more than ten minutes to go around its perimeter – barefoot.

In fact, a vacation on the Maldives is the epitome of 'barefoot luxury.' No explanation is needed for this since you can see it for yourselves (with an emotion that can only be called desire) in the photographs here. What can be said is that the resort in question is the Four Seasons at Landaa Giraavaru, which lies on the island of the same name in the Baa atoll, the only one in the Maldives that has been declared a UNESCO World Biosphere Reserve due to the particularly rich life of its reefs and seabed. Needless to say, it offers all the amenities of a five-star hotel, from those conceived specially for 'romantic idlers' to those who (also) seek adventure. For those who fall in the second category there is the diving center with a resident marine biologist as well as trips on the *dhoni* (the traditional Maldivian boat)

84 - 'Barefoot luxury' is a term for a vacation in the 'magnificent nothing' of the Maldives, where idleness (on enchanting beaches) is a virtue – provided you are a couple.

85 - The Maldives are the dream islands of the collective imagination. There are 1192 of them distributed across 26 atolls, and a seaplane is needed to get to the outermost ones. During your vacation, however, you must explore the ones near the resort on a *dhoni*, a traditional palm-wood boat.

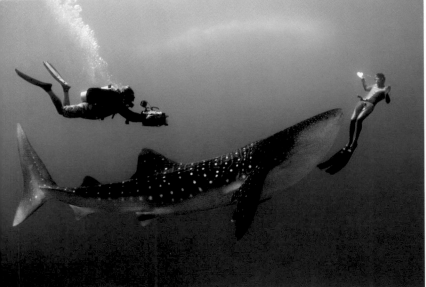

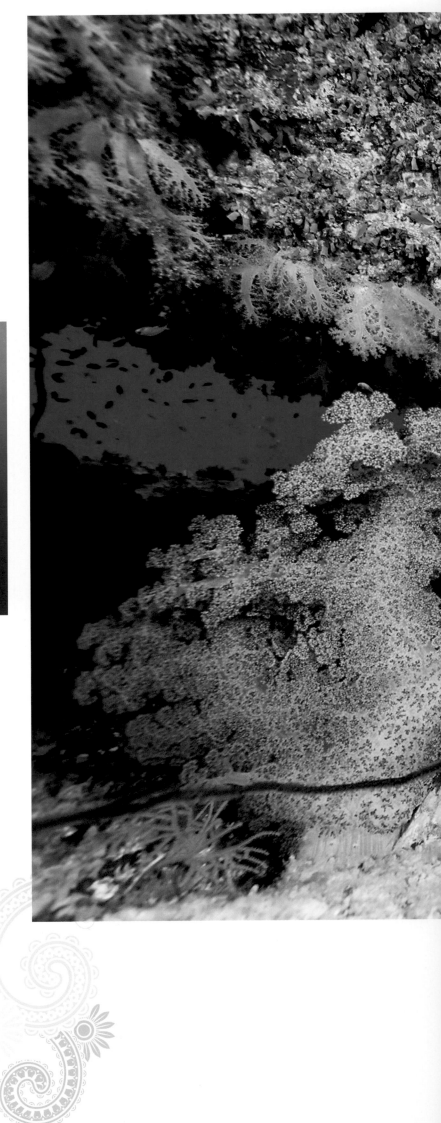

86 - Swimming together with manta rays, whose movements are as graceful as those of ballet dancers, or – for more intrepid visitors – observing sharks from a short distance, are only two of the many thrilling adventures in store for anyone visiting this marvelous archipelago.

86 / 87 - After suffering from the effects of El Niño in 1998, the coral reefs of the Maldives – especially the atolls of Ari and Baa – once again offer a dazzling display of underwater gardens of phenomenal color and a huge fish population.

to the islands inhabited by the local natives, who support themselves with fishing and handicrafts and live in small white houses made of palm-tree wood and coral stone.

In addition, the resort has a luxury catamaran, the *Four Seasons Explorer*, which goes back and forth between Landaa Giravaaru and the island of Kuda Huraa, in the South Male Atoll, offering an unforgettable cruise to the other, equally luxurious resort of this prestigious hotel chain. In this 'magnificent nothing' you should have only one thought in mind: find the right person with whom to share this marvelous experience of the Maldives.

Dubai

United Arab Emirates

In his *Arabian Sands*, the English explorer Wilfred Thesiger relates a terrible experience he had in the summer of 1946, as he was approaching the shores of the Persian Gulf. Without any food and only a canteen of water, he spent three days among the desert dunes suffering from hallucinations while waiting for his Bedouin guide. "No," he wrote, "I would rather be here starving as I was than sitting in a chair, replete with food, listening to the wireless and dependent on cars to take me through Arabia."

Thesiger died in 2003 at the venerable age of 93 and is famous for having grasped, more than any other person, the mystique of emptiness that defines the desert as the symbol of philosophical nothingness. Who knows what he would say today, if at the end of a journey he and his camel should happen upon one of the ten lanes of the Sheikh Zayed Road leading into the city of Dubai, the paradoxical place that could be called a 'full desert.' Thesiger's torrid nightmares would pale at the sight of the Burj Khalifa, the tallest skyscraper in the world; man-made Palm Island, which consists of two palm-tree shaped islands; an artificial archipelago shaped like the world (called, in fact, The World); the Mall of The Emirates, the largest and most inordinately glitzy shopping center on earth; and Ski Dubai, an indoor ski run where one can do a slalom on powdery snow when the outside temperature is 104°. These are only a few of the marvels of the second largest 'Sheikhland' in the United Arab

Emirates. A phantasmagorical branch of the Louvre Museum designed by Jean Nouvel has opened in the capital, Abu Dhabi, while Frank O. Gehry has been commissioned to build a new Guggenheim Museum. We can indubitably view Dubai as a sheikh's dream come true, but can we call it a romantic place for a vacation? First of all, never underestimate the aphrodisiacal power of shopping, at least for the 'better half' of the world. This is a place where you can satisfy the wildest desire, even one you may never have realized you had – be it a candlelight dinner in a tropical aquarium with over 35 million cubic feet of water that is home to 52 species of fish, a cruise at sunset on a luxurious version of the traditional Persian Gulf merchants' sailing vessels. The last-mentioned option in particular is a specialty of the One&Only Royal Mirage hotel, which overlooks magnificent Jumeirah beach and is one of the most exclusive resorts in the Emirates, not only for its architecture, furnishings, and palm tree gardens, which are so luxuriant that they seem to emerge from one of Scheherazade's stories, but also because of the excellent service that meets the guests' every need... and whim. For that matter, having whims is a prerogative of Dubai, a city that offers its citizens a form of excitement that cannot be called anything but sexual. Yes, Dubai is precisely like sex. And, to quote the famous satirist Woody Allen, "Sex without love is a meaningless experience, but as far as meaningless experiences go, it's pretty damn good."

88 / 89 - Facing immense Jumeirah Beach, the One&Only Royal Mirage is the most romantic resort in the United Arab Emirates. All of Dubai, in fact, is a hyperbolical series of Guinness records, the chief of which is the 2716-feet-tall, 160-story Burj Khalifa, the tallest skyscraper in the world. It lies in the very heart of downtown Dubai and is surrounded by areas of greenery and majestic fountains.

Petra

Jordan

The Swiss traveler Ludwig Burckhardt rediscovered the magnificent Nabataean city of Petra in 1812, but the legend of what is one of the most famous archeological sites in the world began in 1838, when a young Scottish artist, David Roberts, went back home after making about 100 sketches and paintings of all its fascinating ruins, thereby triggering an almost obsessive desire to see them among Europeans of the Romantic Era.

This desire is still quite alive now that everybody has seen Petra, so to speak, even before setting foot in Jordan. And yet there are no images – not even ones by the greatest photographers, masters of light effects and ephemeral phenomena – that can prepare us for the true colors of the rocks at Petra – a whirl of reds, oranges, and pinks as fluid as Oriental silk. Likewise, nothing can prepare us for the thrill of arriving – after passing through the narrow, winding Siq canyon that serves as the only access to the city – in front of the extraordinary theatrical setting of the Khazneh al-Farun or Pharaoh's Treasury (or Al Khazneh/Treasury). This is only the beginning of a fabulous itinerary among

dozens of architectural structures – temples, tombs and residences – that constitute nothing less than a miracle, but one that owes a great deal to the grandiosity and poetry of the entire setting, a natural amphitheater of rare splendor.

You will be so satisfied with your tour of Petra that you will desire nothing more. But, as lovers know only too well, desire is fueled by ever new emotions. And Jordan has many in store. The most obvious is a night spent under the stars after dinner in a Bedouin tent in the Wadi Rum, one of the most spectacular valleys in the world, whose myth originated with *The Seven Pillars of Wisdom* by T.E. Lawrence, better known as Lawrence of Arabia. Perhaps the most intriguing thrill is the discovery of unexpected greenery along the narrow Jordan Valley as far as the Dead Sea, or exploring on horseback the gorges of the Wadi Mujib, now a reserve, or a refreshing swim in the falls and Hammamat Zarqa Ma'in hot springs. Near this paradise is a site of historic importance, the ruins of the Mukawir, the palace-stronghold, in which the legendary Salomé danced for King Herod. In this

90 / 91 - Known as 'the Monastery' because its rooms contain crosses carved in the Byzantine period, Al-Deir was built as the tomb of the Nabataean king Obodas I. If this is the most majestic edifice in Petra, certainly the most fascinating is the Khazhneh al-Farun, or 'Pharaoh's Treasury,' which appears as if by magic at the end of the narrow and winding Siq canyon, which offers the only access to the city.

92 - An excursion on camelback among the rock formations of the Wadi Rum, experiencing the thrill of the desert as it was in the time of Lawrence of Arabia.

93 - Not far from the Dead Sea and historic city of Madaba, a narrow valley conceals the oasis of Ma'in, whose hot springs were used by the ancient Romans. Here, in a setting of wild, rugged beauty, is situated the Evason Ma'in Six Senses eco-resort, where guests can indulge in the pleasure of spa treatments.

oasis, which lies in a hollow 866 feet below sea level that blends perfectly with the landscape, lies the recently built Evason Ma'in Hot Springs and Six Senses Spa, the most alluring eco-resort in Jordan, which – and it couldn't be otherwise – boasts an outstanding spa where you can wallow in the pleasure of massages and beauty treatments with Dead Sea salt and mud as well as dates and honey.

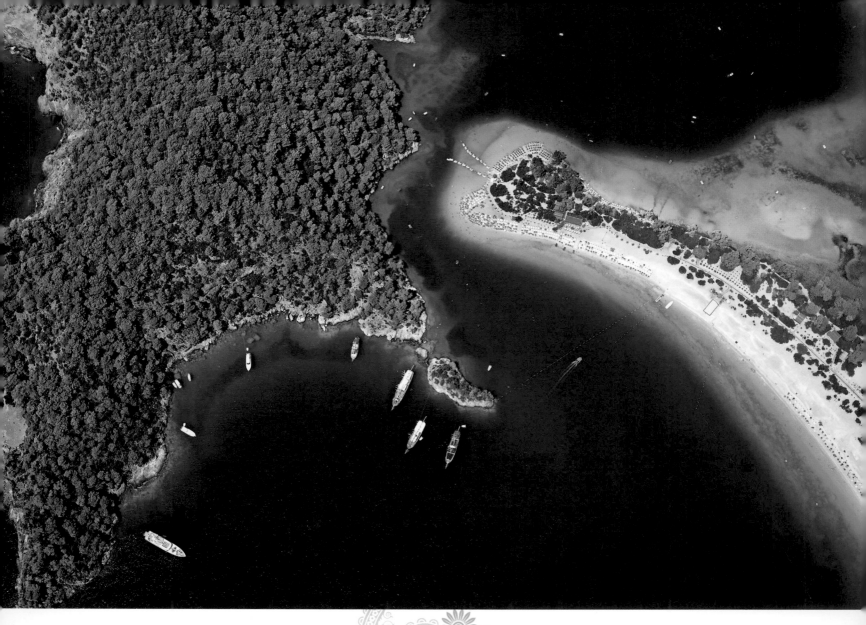

The Turkish Coast

Turkey

94 *top and* **95** - A few nautical miles south of Fethiye, Ölüdeniz ('Dead Sea' in Turkish) owes its name to the fact that its turquoise lagoon, bordered by a strip of fine white sand and cliffs dotted with fragrant pine trees, is well protected from the wind. Besides providing a safe shelter for boats, it offers truly enchanting scenery.

94 *bottom* - An appetizer (with champagne) at sunset while skirting the coast of Turkey on a luxury yacht.

It's impossible not to notice it, with its black sails standing out against the sky as it plows so elegantly through the waters of Turkey's coast. This is the yacht – or *gulet* in Turkish – known as *Beluga One*, which clearly displays, were this necessary, that it is the most precious sailing vessel ever seen in the Mediterranean. Having deservedly earned enthusiastic reviews from prestigious *savoir vivre* hedonist magazines across half the globe, this vessel has been restored and refitted in every detail by the famous London designer Anouskha Hempel. Needless to say, chartering t for a summer cruise is a privilege for a few. If one can do without black sails and a cabin that looks like a sultan's residence, there is good news: even in the luxury category – which includes a waiter and haute-cuisine chef on board – the marvels of the Turk sh coast are something that anyone, or almost anyone, can experience thanks to such charter companies as Exclusive Gulets, which offers a fleet of traditional schooners and caiques (an offshoot of the *tirhandil*, the traditional ancient Aegean sailing boat usec by sponge fishermen and divers) equipped with all sorts of amenities that can satisfy even the most demanding travelers. Moreover, let it be said that the true luxury of a vacation on this sea lies in the beauty of its sites, whether they be Bodrum and Antalya, the queens of the Turkish summer at the two ends of the coastline, or the villages and islets you visit during the trip. Fifty years have passed since caique cruises were organized by a handful of Turkish intellectuals and *bon vivants* inspired by the works of Cevat Şakir Kabaağaçlı, the poet who abandoned Istanbul in 1925 to go live with the sailors of Bodrum and later wrote stories under the pseudonym 'Fisherman of Halicarnassus.' However, a vacation along the Turkish coast also offers the absolute pleasure of being the first to arrive, so to speak, in a deserted bay where you can drop anchor for a night under an amphitheater of stars, or in one of the coves that, according to legend, served as sites for the trysts of Mark Anthony and Cleopatra.

Among the famous sights, magnificent surprises always lie in store in the town of Fethiye, which, founded over the ruins of ancient Themessos, has a particularly fascinating historic area (where, even in August it is worthwhile indulging in the pleasure of the local hammam or Turkish bath, situated in a 16th-century Ottoman structure) and magnificent beaches, such as the famous Ölüdeniz. No less fascinating is Kalkan, the principal center of the Lycian civilization, with the bay of Patara, considered the birthplace of the god Apollo, and Kaş, with its picturesque bazaar and bays dotted with archeological ruins only a few feet beneath the water's surface. Finally, an absolute must are the fishing villages of Çirali and Kemer, where the turquoise sea lies in lovely contrast against the green forest that extends towards the interior as far as the eye can see; lying in Olympos National Park, it seems to remind us that this is a vacation that would have pleased the gods.

Lapland
Sweden

96 - The last wild frontier in Europe, Swedish Lapland is splendid all year long. Yet for those who don't mind the cold, winter is the best season for this is when its snow-clad landscapes are most exciting. Here you can enjoy alpine and cross-country skiing, take adventurous rides on a motor-sled or – in more romantic fashion – on a reindeer- or huskie-drawn sleigh, and thus become acquainted with the traditions and lifestyle of the Sami, the 'natives of the cold.'

97 - Abisko National Park boasts the ultra-modern Aurora Sky Station, an ideal place for observing the magical Northern Lights.

Situated 124 miles north of the Arctic Circle, Jukkasjärvi has a population of 1100 people and 1000 huskies. It is both one of the most remote villages in the Swedish Lapland and, paradoxically, as the northern tip of our planet, the warmest attraction during the winter. In fact, 50,000 tourists from 80 different nations have spent at least one night in the famous Ice Hotel.

Open from December to mid-April, when the spring thaw turns the ice into liquid, the hotel is assembled between late October and November by a team of 100 peoples from a substance that has been christened *snice* (a combination of snow and ice). 2500 blocks of ice weighing 5000 tons are gathered from the nearby Thorne River over the preceding year.

Once the supporting structure is completed over an area encompassing 59,201 square feet, a group of artists and designers arrive at the scene to sculpt the furnishings, the suites, and the communal areas, which include a church that has been made on request and is quite often used for weddings.

However magical and magnificent the rooms in their gleaming white hues may be, sleeping under a hide in one of the alcoves of the Ice Hotel at a temperature of − 5° Celsius (23° Fahrenheit) is quite a test of stamina (and love) that requires a 'survival course,' which is held every evening by the hotel staff.

So far, however, all the guests have passed the test with honors, and truth be said, if they suffered from shivers or had trouble falling asleep it was due, if anything, to the thrill of being there. In the morning, after a large breakfast that includes warm whortleberry juice, the many activities offered will make your vacation in Lapland even more extraordinary, if that is possible.

You can choose from adventurous rides in motor- or dog sleds, visits to Sami villages, or cross-country snowshoe treks along the Kungsleden or King's Trail (275 miles long and the most exciting winter circuit in Sweden) in Abisko National Park.

Covering an area of only 30 square miles, this park protects a wild, cold territory that is considered the best spot in Swedish Lapland to see the Northern Lights.

In order to enjoy this fantastic nocturnal experience you must go to the Aurora Sky Station – finally a warm place! – with its state-of-the-art observatory and romantic restaurant featuring gourmet Arctic cuisine.

98 - A unicorn and Gothic architecture: fantasy dominates the hall, but each year the Ice Hotel is built from scratch, always different and always absolutely phenomenal.

99 *top* - Five degrees below zero Celsius: this is the temperature of the ice alcoves in the Ice Hotel. Yet, surprisingly, a soft fur blanket and good company are all you need to spend a dreamy night.

99 *bottom* - Five thousand tons of ice are needed to build the Ice Hotel; besides its fabulous suites, the complex also houses a church often used for weddings.

Saint Petersburg

Russia

100 - A common sight in this splendid city only 497 miles from the Arctic Circle is snow, which makes its architecture seem even more fantastic, from the Cathedral of Smolny – next to which stands the first public girls' school in the Russian Empire – to the Admiralty, with its bold gilded spire that serves as a sort of hub for the city's three main arteries: Nevsky Prospekt, Voznesensky Prospekt and the Gorokhovaia Street.

101 - The 1640-ft façade of the Winter Palace (which houses the Hermitage Museum) is reflected in the frozen snow.

You may really feel like dancing when looking at *The Dance*, painted for a Russian nobleman by Henri Matisse, who chose to represent the rhythm and spirit of the 20th century with the motif of a round dance. This is only one of the many exquisite masterpieces in the Hermitage, the world's largest museum with 2.7 million works of art housed in 400 rooms inside 6 buildings, which include the main residence of the Russian czars, the amazing Winter Palace, with its brilliant combination of gilding and stucco. Next come the exciting bursts of colors in the canvases of Chagall, Kandinsky and Malevich at the Russian State Museum, or the multi-colored onion dome of the Church of the Savior of the Spilt Blood, the only truly Russian architectural structure in the entire city.

It is impossible to count – much less visit during a short vacation – all the treasures in St. Petersburg, the most extraordinary city in Mother Russia, which, conceived in the early 18th century by Peter the Great, became a reality thanks to a group of fine Italian architects. It is equally impossible to follow the tracks of all the great interpreters of Russian culture,

from Pushkin to Dostoevsky, or listen to all the music of Tchaikovsky and Stravinsky (you would have to book a seat at the Mariinsky Theater every night). Another impossible feat would be to see and grasp all the beauty of St. Petersburg beyond the city. Here lie the country residences of the Romanov dynasty, from the Peterhof Grand Palace, the garden of which is embellished with no fewer than 140 gilt fountains, to Tsarskoye Selo, a town boasting an imperial residence with an extremely long flamboyant Baroque facade – a painted dream of turquoise, white, and gold and an interior that is the essence of lavishness – for the use of rulers such as Catherine the Great. To see all this, the days would have to be even longer than those that get brighter and turn into the famous White Nights as summer arrives in this town merely 500 miles from the Arctic Circle.

Indeed, in St. Petersburg even establishments devoted to relaxation and recreation are cultural. For example, the Astoria, the hotel in which you simply must stay, was founded in an opulent building opposite St. Isaac's Cathedral before the October Revolution.

Magnificently restored, it has hosted the public and private exploits of many famous personalities. It was here that the hot-headed Rasputin had trysts with his mistresses and Isadora Duncan danced barefoot in salons. Many European rulers have come to the hotel's boutique, which features the jewelry of Fabergé as well as his eggs, the most precious in the world. If you stay at the Astoria, a cup of Russian tea poured from a samovar or a romantic dinner featuring Beluga caviar will make you feel as though you have truly entered a fairy tale of the czars.

102 *top* - Situated on Griboedov Canal, the Church of the Savior of Spilled Blood is the only truly typical Russian building in the city. The onion domes and walls are covered with about 75,000 square feet of mosaics.

102 *bottom* - The opulent Hotel Astoria offers a fine view of St. Isaac's Square. Inaugurated a short time before the October Revolution – which brought down the curtain on czarist St. Petersburg – the hotel is an urban legend that has hosted celebrities – from members of royal families to legendary actors and even intriguing spies.

103 *top* - Comparable to Versailles with regard to opulence, Peterhof is also known as the 'city of fountains' – 137 of them, plus four waterfalls, the most majestic of which flows before the main façade of the royal palace.

103 *bottom* - The Ballroom, also known as the Grand Hall or Hall of Lights, is the most grandiose space in the so-called Golden Enfilade of the Catherine Palace at Tsarskoye Selo. It boasts an astounding, spectacularly painted ceiling.

The Sunnmøre Alps
Norway

104 - Traversed by the swiftly flowing Valldøla River, which abounds in fish, the Vallsal region in the Sunnmøre Alps is a special place for hiking and trekking in an idyllic winter setting. These mountains, dotted with farms and tiny villages (and ideal for cross-country or off-piste skiing) offer panoramic views of the Geirangerfjord, the jewel of this famous region of fjords.

105 - Hi-tech minimalism in the marvelous rooms of the Juvet landscape hotel make for an unforgettable 'mountain Robinson Crusoe' experience.

Because of its ethereal beauty it has been called Brudesløret or Bridal Veil. This is just one of the spectacular waterfalls that plunge into the Geirangerfjord, the most precious gem in the crown of Norwegian fjords. Together with Sju Systre or Seven Sisters – so named because of the seven 'arms' that spill into the huge body of water with a deafening roar, creating fantastic rainbows in the sunlight – this is one of the most impressive of the long list of marvels that visitors can see during a cruise in the fjord region. But while the view from the waters of the Geirangerfjord is an experience for everyone, so to speak, a more unusual one is the discovery of this part of Norway from on high. This can be done by venturing into the Sunnmøre Alps, which have natural terraces with commanding views of the fjords and of captivating scenery featuring birch and beech woods as well as peaks and valleys that conceal old abandoned farmsteads.

In the Sunnmøre Alps – or more precisely, in the Vallsal zone, traversed by the swift Valldøla River, which abounds in fish, one of the natural features 'responsible' for the magic of the many waterfalls – the most idyllic resort is Juvet, the first landscape hotel on earth, a spot in a virgin mountain setting perfect for a 'Robinson Crusoe.' The product of an ingenious idea concocted by Knut Slinning, a legendary Norwegian alpine guide

and promoter of the *Nasjonale Turistveger* or National Tourist Routes – a network of roads with facilities that criss-cross the entire country – the landscape hotel is a place where the minimalist concept of "less is more" has, so to speak, been taken to an extreme.

Why furnish a hotel room when nature is the most perfect designer imaginable? Consequently, the Juvet hotel – which boasts a rate of zero-emission is composed of a dozen wooden huts with glass walls. The interior holds only a bed, light to read by, and a chaise longue in which to relax, all magnificently 'decorated' with the blue of the sky and the river, the green of the trees, and the grey of the mountain. And, of course, the brilliant white of the snow in winter. Surprisingly, however, the hotel is anything but spartan. It has a top-quality restaurant and a nature spa. An 'extreme' luxury, above all, however are the activities that can be enjoyed in the surroundings in every season under the skillful guidance of Knut Slinning himself. You can hike along the path named after the heroic Viking monarch Olav Haraldsson or walk down the Trollstigen or Troll Road, which leads to a rocky spur that affords a view of the fjord and the quaint town of Åndalsnes, at the base of a 3281-foot-tall rockface. You can also go rafting and canyoning, fish for salmon, or ski even in summer and off-piste, in the magical setting of the Jostedal glacier.

The Scottish Highlands
United Kingdom

106 - An old-time romantic trip aboard the *Jacobite*, a steam train that runs from Fort William to Port Mallaigh by way of vertiginous viaducts through the green landscape of the Scottish Highlands. Once you've reached your destination, your best bet is to spend the night at the Ardanaseig, a luxury hotel in a lovely 19th-century country mansion designed by the legendary Scottish architect William Burn.

107 - Near Nairn is Cawdor Castle, known for its splendid gardens and connection to Shakespeare's tragedy *Macbeth*.

Every September at least one member of the Royal Family is present at the most important event of the Highland Games, held in Braemar, Aberdeenshire. Ever since 1820, in the wake of the interest raised by Romantic authors (Sir Walter Scott, first and foremost) in Scottish history and tradition, and thanks to the royal patronage of Queen Victoria, these 'Olympic Games in a kilt' have been granted official status. All the same, the spirit of their medieval origins and their spontaneity live on, as does the excitement of watching the various events – the caber toss, wrestling, Scottish hammer throw, stone put, and uphill foot race – to the musical accompaniment of bagpipes. What is more, foreigners are invited to participate.

This is only logical, for you need spend only a couple of days in the Highlands – the region that descends from the mountains and turns into a land of hills and lakes towards the northwestern coast and islands of this proud nation – to feel Scottish and part of a world that still seems to be living in a legendary, heroic age. This is the Scotland of the collective imagination, which should be explored slowly by car and partly on foot to the wildest destinations, such as the paths of Ben Nevis, the

tallest mountain in the British Isles. Or you can travel by rail, especially on the *Jacobite*, the steam train that runs from Fort William, the main town in the Highlands, to the coastal city of Mallaigh along vertiginous viaducts and through land that is so magical that it served as the location of certain cult scenes in the Harry Potter film series.

This is an itinerary filled with mystery, culture and romance, and as such cannot fail to include visits to the fabulous castles of Scotland. Urquahrt Castle on the banks of Loch Ness, the lake famous for its 'monster,' offers dramatic and breathtaking views. Ballindalloch, in Banffshire, is the classic fairy-tale castle, known as the 'Pearl of the North' for its architecture, lavish furnishings and rooms, and an extraordinary collection of paintings. You must go to the Castle of Mey in Caithness in the afternoon, just in time for high tea (as it also has one of the most elegant tearooms in the United Kingdom). Surrounded by an idyllic park, it was the favorite summer residence of the Queen Mother. And sunset is the right time – partly because you can have a taste of its legendary pure malt whisky at that hour – to take in the literary references of the Castle of Cawdor, which is associated with

108 - The picturesque ruins of the 14th-century Castle of Urquart stands majestically on one shore of the Loch Ness, certainly the most famous and photographed site in the Highlands.

108 / 109 - The ancestral residence of the Campbell clan, Kilchurn Castle seems to emerge magically from Loch Awe. When the level of the lake rises, the promontory of the castle turns into an island.

Shakespeare's tragedy *Macbeth*. The county of Argyllshire, on the other hand, offers you the Castle of Kilburn, a 15th-century turreted fortification, which is the most picturesque and frequently photographed ruin in the region; with the morning mist, it seems to emerge miraculously from the waters of Loch Awe. And if you wish to experience the most magical of Scottish nights along the banks of this lake, you must book a room at the Ardanaiseig, a grandiose 19th-century country manor and the most romantic hotel in the Highlands.

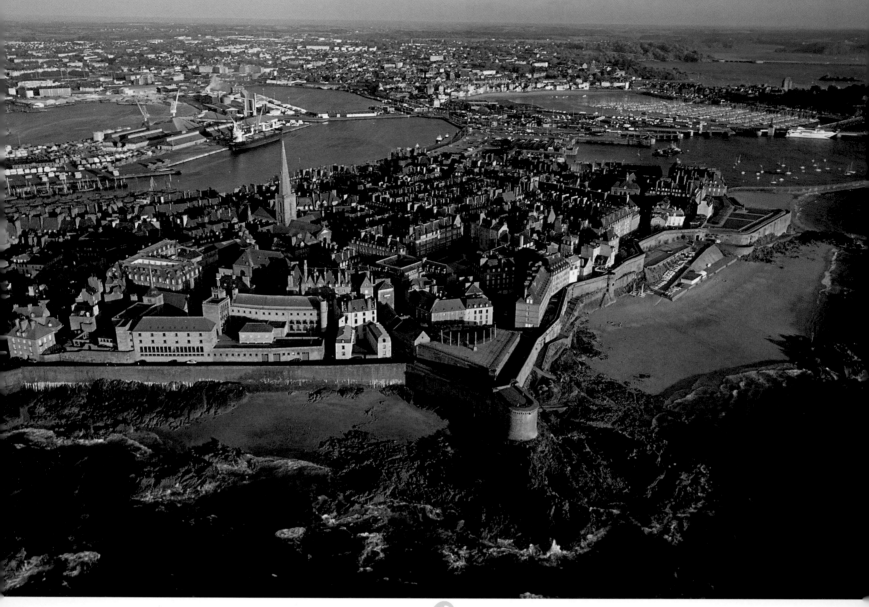

Saint-Malo

France

110 - "A crown of stones placed on the waves;" an aerial view proves that this description of Saint-Malo is extraordinarily apt. This old city is a starting point for any trip eastward and up the coast toward Cancale, along which you can experience the wild charm of Brittany. Another attraction at Saint-Malo is Château Richeux, a romantic hotel in a typical Breton mansion, a *malouinière*, which offers all kinds of amenities and leisure activities.

111 - In Cancale, the oyster capital of France, the beds of these precious mollusks extend along the shore as far as the eye can see.

In the first century AD, the Roman historian Pliny called Brittany "the spectator of the Ocean," thus synthesizing the physical and symbolic position of this land as well as its future history and fate in an unusual manner. Arguably there is no other land in the world where the presence of the sea seems so overpowering in its variations as in this magnificent and singular region of France. Here the sea always dominates the landscape, making it wild and romantic, as well as harsh and disturbing, somewhere between reality and myth. And in all of Brittany there is no other city like Saint-Malo, which seems to have been born of the ocean. As Flaubert wrote, this city, "built right on the ocean and… enclosed by ramparts, looks like a crown of stones, the gems of which are the machicolations."

Built entirely of granite, which grants it an impressive architectural unity and compactness, Saint-Malo is perched on its famous massive ramparts that epitomize its independent, tenacious, and war-like spirit. Renowned as the city of pirates in the service of the king of France – and thus considered a 'wasps' nest' by its English enemies – this gray and austere city with its obscure and magnetic charm is the birthplace of the author considered the father of Romanticism, François-René de Chateaubriand (1768-1848). In the 17th and 18th century, it became the principal port of France, flourishing thanks to the fishing industry

and commerce of spices, cloth, and slaves from the Indies, as well as pirates' booty. It was then that the ship owners and captains of Saint-Malo constructed the so-called *Malouinières*, splendid country villas (always a stone's throw from the sea), which surround the crown of the fortified city and add to it an air of sweet harmony. One of these has become a *hôtel de charme et de caractère*, which, given its name, Château de Colombier, or Dovecote Castle, is ideal for romantic trysts.

It is sheer joy to return to this 'doves' shelter' every evening after spending the day enjoying the beaches, sky, and splendid towns along the Emerald Coast of Brittany. One of these is Dinard, the sophisticated sister of Saint-Malo, which by the mid-19th century had already earned the title of Cannes of the North for its elegance and upper-class visitors. Among these many celebrities was Picasso, who spent some time here painting his famous and sensual *Baigneuse* (Bather), and film director Eric Rohmer, who shot one of his masterpieces, *A Summer's Tale*, in Saint-Malo – a disturbing tale of love and betrayal that seems to follow the rhythm of the violent tides between the beach of l'Écluse and the cliffs of Sentier des Douaniers. The latter, a seaside footpath laid out by customs officers over 100 years ago in an attempt to block smuggling across the British Channel, is an absolute must for a wonderful walk

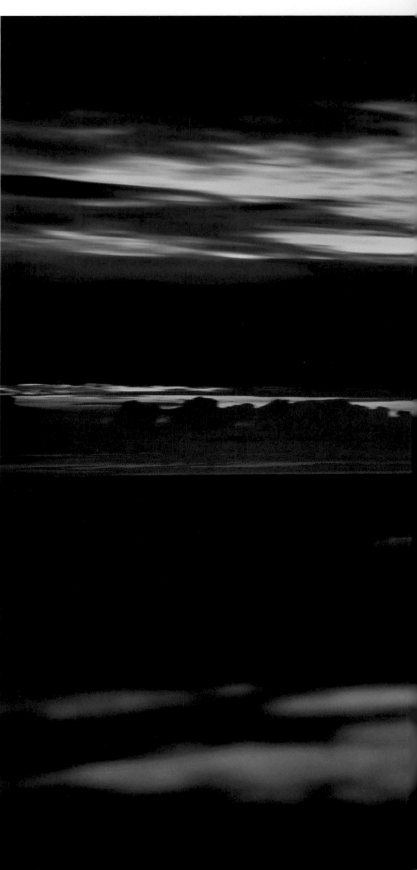

112 - "Welcome aboard," says the sign on one of the characteristic oyster bars along Cancale's marina, where customers can indulge in a dozen oysters accompanied by a glass of ice-cold Muscadet.

112 / 113 - Cancale is a step away from Normandy, where a major attraction is the spectacle of mystical Mont-Saint-Michel and its bay at sunset.

at sunset, delightful when the sea and cliffs blaze with unreal colors and the wind makes the clouds dance. And eastward, towards Normandy (and Mont-Saint-Michel), is another 'must' offering more prosaic pleasures: Cancale, the picturesque maritime village that boasts the title of world capital of the oyster, the quintessential aphrodisiac. This delicacy must be enjoyed at Le Coquillage, the gourmet restaurant run by the celebrated chef Oliver Roellinger and which is part of a romantic and relaxing hotel with its own large kitchen garden, the Château R cheux, situated in a large 1920s villa overlooking the rocks and the sea.

Champagne
France

"In victory I deserve it, in defeat I need it." This was what Winston Churchill liked to say about champagne, which the great British politician considered one of life's greatest joys. With sharp wit and irony, on the other hand, the author Oscar Wilde associated its bubbles with the sparks of passion, noting that "in married households the champagne is rarely of a first-rate brand." Legend has it that Abbot Dom Pérignon – credited, perhaps erroneously, with the invention of the *methode champenoise* in 1670 – urged his confrères to taste the first glass of champagne while shouting: "Come quickly, I'm drinking the stars!"

Champagne is a nectar with the magical power to provide that 'something extra' for any special occasion. There is no better special occasion than spending a few days – ideally in autumn, during the grape harvest – in the region where the most seductive wine of all is produced. Situated 93 miles from Paris, this area traversed by the Marne River is invites you to follow an itinerary that has to begin at Hautvillers Abbey,

where you can visit Dom Perignon's grave, then proceed to Reims. This is the charming principal city of the Champagne region, where you can admire the world-famous gothic cathedral of Notre Dame, where the French kings were crowned, and which is now adorned with marvelous stained-glass windows by Marc Chagall, as well as a historic center that offers a fascinating gamut of architectural styles, from Gallo-Roman to Art Déco. The city is also the home to some of the most famous houses of Champagne, such as Veuve Clicquot, Mumm, Ruinart, Tattinger and Pommery. The winery of the last of these is a neo-gothic, neo-Elizabethan chateau built in the late 19th century to attract British customers. Each house offers visits to caves hewn out of chalk rock and a tasting session of the grand *crus*. Not far from Reims city center is Le Domaine les Crayères, the most extraordinary relais et château in France, deservedly called 'little Versailles' because of its lavish furnishings and the utter elegance of its restaurant, which boasts a wine list of over 300 labels of the best

114

114 - World-famous Moët et Chandon champagne is stored in the largest group of wine cellars in Épernay, the capital of this immensely popular sparkling wine. The cellars are cut out of rock and form a labyrinth of galleries that run for 17 miles and contain hundreds of thousands of bottles. The firm offers guided tours that conclude with a sampling of sensational crus.

115 - The marvelous vineyards in this region produce over 52 million gallons of champagne every year.

champagne producers. After a night that will certainly be sparkling, you can continue your trip – by car, bicycle or one of the *bateau* that goes up the Marne River – to the picturesque villages scattered among the vineyards, until you reach Épernay, a town of 26,000 souls that is the champagne capital. Indeed, its caves consist of no fewer than 68 miles of rock-hewn tunnels storing a treasure of 200 million bottles, while the famous Avenue de Champagne is lined with the wineries of Moët et Chandon, Perrier Jouët, Mercier, and Pol Roger, to name only a few. All of them are well worth a visit, but more adventurous souls should stop by the small Maison Leclers-Briant winery;after a 'speleological' descent into the cave, aided by a fixed rope, you can watch the age-old ritual of *sabrage*, when bottles are opened with a slash of a sword.

116 - Surrounded by a 7-hectare park, Domaine Les Crayères is a short distance from Reims. Because of its architectural beauty, opulent furnishings, and sophisticated atmosphere, this very special hotel has come to be known as 'little Versailles.'

117 *top* - In bar La Rotonde at Domaine les Crayères, guests can sip a glass of the famous bubbles and admire the magnificent green landscape.

117 *bottom* - One of the elegant rooms in the hotel, which guarantees a magical and sparkling night – just like champagne.

The Loire Valley

France

118 - Along the banks of the Loire River lies the romantic hamlet of Amboise, dominated by the Château d'Amboise, which played a leading role in the history of France and also exerted great influence on the politics and art of Renaissance Europe. The fabulous and highly romantic château of Azay-le-Rideau – one of the most famous and popular castles in the Loire region – on the other hand, lies on an island in the middle of the Indre River.

119 - A masterpiece of Renaissance architecture, Chambord is the largest château in the Loire region yet seems almost ethereal in the morning mist.

In France they say that the Seine is the bride of Paris but the Loire is its lover. As a lover – of power, that is – it has witnessed intrigues, bitter rivalries, massacres, and thrones built and destroyed. So much so that if one retraces all the events that took place down its banks it becomes obvious that great history has always made stops along the longest river in France. Moreover, as a lover – of beauty – it has châteaux that can be matched in no other place, structures that blend in perfectly with a landscape that accompanies the river on its 620-mile course that breaks up into a multitude of streams and canals, among forests, vineyards, gardens, and, here and there, villages and cities of the province that is a tangible manifestation of the expression *la douce France*.

Along the stretch between Orléans and the region of Touraine, the Loire and its tributaries become what is known as the 'Valley of the Kings,' which casts a spell on all those who travel there among its most famous châteaux. One of these is the Château de Chambord, a 16th-century *folie de grandeur* of King Francis I, which, lying on the Cloisson River, overwhelms viewers both because of its exterior – a dizzy fantasy of chimneys, towers, and loggias – and its interior, with its 440 rooms and a monumental double staircase that displays the genius of the person who may have designed it, Leonardo da Vinci. There is also the Château de Blois, which boasts a collection of 3000 works of art and served as the residence of Henry IV and Marguerite de Valois, who married for purely political convenience. It was here that the king ordered the assassination of the Duke of Guise, the first and most influential of the many lovers of the woman who went down in history as the passionate Queen Margaret of France. Further down the valley you can visit the fairy-tale Château de Chaumont-sur-Loire, which offered hospitality to many astrologers, including Nostradamus, and the Château d'Amboise, which still belongs to the Count of Paris, a direct descendant of the royal house of France. From here the Loire Valley opens out towards Tours, where you must make a detour to admire the exceptional Château de Chenonceau, bound to the tale of rivalry between Diane de Poitiers and Caterina de' Medici, the lover and wife, respectively, of Henry II. While the seductive atmosphere of the castle and the garden evokes the passions of Diane, the commission to construct the romantic Grand Gallery on the bridge over the Cher River, can be credited to Caterina. The nearby Château Villandry also has an utterly feminine allure, which is strongly felt in the perfect labyrinth of its Renaissance gardens, the most beautiful in the region. Among the many other fabulous buildings, mention must be made of the Castle Azay-le-Rideau, which Balzac compared to "a diamond of many facets in a setting of the Indre," and the austere Château Angers, home of the immense 14th-century masterpiece known as the Apocalypse Tapestry.

Finally, lying a short distance from the massive walls of Angers is one of the most extraordinary of the many castles that have been converted into hotels, the Château des Briottières, owned by the same aristocratic family for six generations. It was built in the 15th but reconstructed in the 18th century, when it was converted ito a *maison de délices* or house of delights. Its huge park is an invitation for romantic strolls, and its lavishly furnished suites offer an invitation to live... like the Loire. That is, like lovers.

120 *top* - The Grand Gallery is one of the jewels of the Château de Chenonceau, which lies over the Cher River and was built at the behest of Caterina de' Medici with splendid gardens commissioned by Diane de Poitiers. The castle thus captures the rivalry between these two *grande dames*.

120 *bottom* - A romantic boat trip to the fabulous Château de Chaumont-sur-Loire.

121 - Lying in an enchanting park near Angers, the Château des Briottières has been converted into a delightful and elegant hotel.

Die Romantische Strasse

Germany

122 - Built in the 19th century to please the eccentric fantasy of King Ludwig II of Bavaria, Neuschwanstein Castle seems to be made of phantasmagorical material as its crenelated towers dominate a hill in Schwangau. Not far from it lies a fine hotel – not surprisingly called the König Ludwig Hotel – with a spa and pools overlooking the fabulous landscape.

123 - Autumn colors begin to enhance the Bavarian Alps around Füssen, which because of its proximity to Neuschwanstein and Hohenschwangau Castles, is the most popular destination on the Romantische Strasse, a road laid out in 1950 so that the Germans could rediscover the beauty and history of their country.

Cinderella and Prince Charming lived happily ever after in this, the most romantic fairy-tale castle of all, with its crenellated towers that, like the girl's famous glass slipper, glisten in the sunlight and dominate a magnificent landscape of woods from on high. All young girls dream of experiencing a fairy-tale love story in a place such as this, just as the child in every adult should have the gift of a vacation in the area of the castle that Walt Disney used as the setting for his movie Cinderella.

The castle is Neuschwanstein, conceived by the eccentric fantasy of Ludwig II of Bavaria, known as the Fairy Tale King. In it the throne room is decorated with a phantasmagoria of gold and pseudo-medieval motifs, while the interior of the royal alcove – decorated with frescoes representing another legendary love story, that of Tristan and Iseult – is even more magical than the exterior, if that is possible. Together with the neighboring castle, Hohenschwangau, situated in a panoramic site overlooking the Alpsee and Schwansee lakes, Neuschwanstein is the high point of a route that you can travel by car or bicycle along the Romantische Strasse, the romantic road that runs from the Alps to the banks of the River Main, or more precisely, from the village of Füssen in the south to Würtzburg in the north, and which offers the most magical landscapes and historic towns and sights in Bavaria and Baden-Württemberg along a course of 248 miles. Romantische Strasse is obviously true to its meaning because of the castles – so much so that it deserves another equally romantic stopover at the luxurious König Ludwig Spa Hotel,

in the village of Schwangau. The entire route is a succession of sweet images, delightful villages such as Dinkelsbuhl, Landsberg, and Rothenburg with houses whose trellises are covered with geraniums, and the hills carpeted with the vineyards of Franconia. And let us not forget the pleasure of fine food, because here even the dumplings, spätzle (egg noodles), pies and cakes are gifts of love. It is simply impossible to list all the romantic sights along the 'Romantic Road,' but the musts include Augsburg, the 'city of bankers' with many Roman ruins, and the bucolic region of Pfaffenwinkel – literally 'Priests' Corner' – which boasts nearly 200 churches and religious structures, perhaps the most interesting of which – Weiskirke – lies in the village of Steingaden. On the UNESCO World Heritage List as the most exhilarating example of German rococo, this church is a triumph of gilded and pastel-colored stucco framing a very old and miraculous wooden statue of Christ, which celebrates sacred love with unusual gaiety. At the end of this exciting asphalt road, on the other hand, is the Würzburger Residenz, designed by Balthasar Neumann, a leading German Baroque architect, with the aim of consecrating the glory of the prince-bishops of this lovely city. Enclosed in an Italian-style garden, this palace has exceptional frescoes painted by another genius of the Baroque, Giambattista Tiepolo. His admirable perspective and trompe l'oeils depict extraordinarily vivid representations of mythological figures in grandiose scenes – a hymn to the inevitable temptations of profane love.

St. Moritz
Switzerland

"Sparkling like champagne:" this is how the tourist office of St. Moritz advertises the air one breathes in the pearl of the Engadine Valley in Switzerland, which is surrounded by peaks such as the Piz Bernina, 13,123 feet above sea level and dotted with a group of romantic alpine lakes. It also guarantees 322 days of sun per year in the valley. However, it is not only the altitude and unique scenic beauty that cause the air to have the same inebriating effect as champagne bubbles. Much more important is the inimitable glamor of St. Moritz, exhibited like a flag; indeed, the very name of this resort town is protected by copyright.

St. Moritz was the first exclusive ski resort in the Alps and the only one that has hosted the Winter Olympic Games twice, way back in 1924 and 1948. And though in recent times it hosts more Russian magnates and Arab sheiks than members of European high society, its fame as the queen of the Alps seems to be impermeable to changing fashions and taste. The secret of its perennial success lies in a felicitous mixture of sophistication based on elegance and class (a must

for visitors in February is the White Turf horse race held on a frozen lake, the 'white' equivalent of the famous Ascot racecourse), chic chalets, hotels, and restaurants, and many stylish boutiques that enjoy what can only be called cult popularity. It was here, for example, that Cartier chose to open its first jewelry shop in Switzerland. And while this fact may be a form of veiled advice regarding a gift that could make your vacation even more unforgettable (if that is possible), you should know that the environs of St. Moritz offer unbelievably romantic sights, with mountain scenery that can be enjoyed while skiing (or, in the summer, while taking a fine mountain hike) and quaint villages such as nearby Pontresina, with its delightful old and traditional houses decorated with frescoes. What is more, St. Moritz is the starting point of the Glacier Express, the train that takes eight hours to pass through the most famous localities in Switzerland until it finally reaches the last stop, Zermatt, at the foot of the Matterhorn. Considered the world's most spectacular and romantic train trip, its route allows passengers to admire glaciers and 28 peaks, each

124 / 125 - The outdoor lounge area of the luxurious Chedi Andermatt, a new resort that combines the magical alpine scenery of Switzerland with a contemporary chic style inspired by Oriental models. As for St. Moritz, seen here in a surreal nocturnal view, it is the classic, beautiful mountain resort. Its charm lies in a highly successful marriage of elegant worldliness, fine gourmet dining, luxury shopping, and winter sports.

are over 13,000 feet high, and passes through 91 tunnels and over 291 bridges over deep ravines. And, regardless of whether you heed the advice to pay a visit to the Cartier shop, here is another tip: get off the train at Andermatt, the latest exclusive Swiss ski resort, and enjoy a stay at the Chedi, a new ultra-luxury hotel that has succeeded in its apparently impossible mission to combine alpine scenery and a chic contemporary style that captures the allure of Asia.

126 / 127 - The Glacier Express is the most famous train in the world. It can get you from St. Moritz to Zermatt (or Davos) in about 8 hours, skirting impressive peaks, and traversing remarkable valleys, passing through 91 tunnels and over 291 high-altitude bridges.

126 *bottom* - Snowboard buffs have remarkable runs at their disposal in the Swiss Alps. At St. Moritz the winter cult event is the White Turf, a horse race on a frozen lake that rivals the Ascot racecourse in elegance and glamor.

Megève
France

128 / 129 - With 276 miles of ski runs and 107 lift facilities, the Megève ski resort is among the most exciting in all of the Alps. Yet people do not come here only to ski as there are so many other interesting things to do, such as take a hike to visit the 14 18th-century Calvary chapels, from Mègeve to Mont d'Arbois, nestled among idyllic, beautiful scenery.

128 *bottom* - Every year in the second half of January the snow at Mègeve plays host to the Grande Odysée Savoie Mont Blanc, a dog sled race over a 248-mile route that lasts 10 days.

Christened *Evasion Mont-Blanc*, this is a ski resort that offers a fabulous area for this sport at an altitude ranging from 2350 to 7710 feet and comprising Megève, La Giettaz, Combloux, Saint Gervais, Saint Nicolas and Les Contamines along with 276 miles of slopes and 107 lift facilities. And yet, as hard as one tries, it is impossible to find anyone among the habitués of Megève who spends his or her vacation here only to ski. In the heart of the Haute-Savoie region, the most sophisticated resort in the Alps has been called "the XXI arrondissement of Paris" and offers, in miniature form, all the art necessary to living the good life typical of the French capital. For that matter, unlike its rivals (from Chamonix to St. Moritz and Cortina), Megève has an aristocrat, a tailor, and an architect as the leading personalities of its history instead of alpine guides or legendary skiing champions. The first of these is the Baroness Noémie de Rothschild, who, in 1926, arrived in this champagne-goblet shaped valley with the aim of creating the first exclusive ski resort for upper-class tourism. The second person is Henry Jacques Le Même, who, shortly after earning his degree in architecture, modeled his first vacation home upon Savoie farmhouses. Widening the windows, adding terraces, enlarging rooms and converting the stable into a storeroom for skis and boots, he built the first chalet to be used for typical alpine delights and leisure. While it was being finished, a local tailor,

Armand Allard, made the first *pantalons sauteurs*, trousers that later became thoroughly identified with *fuseaux* (tight-fitting pants), which, fastened around the heel, became the new elegant and aerodynamic style for ski suits.

The rest is history. By 1950, there were already 100 luxury chalets similar to Madame Rothschild's in Megève alone, and at least 30 boutiques that set the guidelines for fashionable ski and snow gear. Since then, things have risen to a crescendo. The year 1963 marked the arrival of Hollywood glamor with Megève serving as the location of the delightful cult film *Charade*, starring Audrey Hepburn and Cary Grant. Today Megève has 90 gourmet restaurants with many Michelin stars, and offers its guests abundant activities besides skiing, including winter golfing on a snow-clad course with a fine panoramic view as well as romantic adventures in a hot-air balloon. But above all, Megève has earned a host of stars in the field of mountain accommodations, the most faithful to the traditional style being Les Fermes de Marie, a romantic oasis that grew out of a masterful restoration of eight old Savoie chalets. The sheep pen has been replaced by a wonderful pool, the granary is now home to the most renowned restaurant in Mègeve, and each room exudes the aura of a luxury mountain refuge in which you can spend fabulous evenings and nights warmed by the blazing fireplace. And by love.

130 - It is impossible not to be spellbound by the perfect Savoyard style of Les Fermes de Marie chalets, with their wooden walls, eternally lit fireplaces, traditional furnishings, and warm colors, — the quintessence of an alpine resort in a romantic, deluxe version.

131 *top* - After spending the day skiing, guests at Les Fermes de Marie are treated to a snack of tea and delicious homemade cake. Then comes a moment of sheer relaxation at the spa or an invigorating swim in the resort pool, which affords a magnificent view of the village and nearby ski runs.

131 *bottom* - Les Fermes de Marie is the result of a fine and imaginative restoration of a group of Savoyard sheep folds, stables, and barns.

Cortina d'Ampezzo
Italy

"They can be white as snow, yellow as the sun, grey as the clouds, pink as roses, black as burnt wood, red as blood... And despite all this, what color are they to those looking from the bottom of their valleys? White? Yellow? Grey? Mother of pearl? Is it ash? a silver hue? Or the pallor of a corpse? Is it a rosey pink? Are they stones or clouds? Are they real or is this a dream?" The lines above were written by Dino Buzzati, one of the leading figures of 20th-century Italian literature, as he observed the ever-changing and unforgettable spectacle of the Dolomites, the mountains, which – as Le Corbusier, another great personality of the last century, once stated – are "the most beautiful architectural work in the world."

In 2010, UNESCO placed them on its World Heritage List for their unique beauty. One cannot deny that the Dolomites are marvelous as a whole. Yet their enchanting beauty also lies in the profiles of their individual peaks, as well as in each of their valleys and villages. Surely vacationers have an especially fond memory of a particular place or sight among these mountains. And once again, are the Dolomites at their best in winter or in summer? Here too it is a question of taste, of feeling.

What is certain for many reasons, however, is that the title 'Queen of the Dolomites' belongs to Cortina d'Ampezzo in any season. It was no coincidence that the famous Dolomites Road, opened in 1909, was laid out to connect the cities of Bolzano and Cortina; that in 1956, the first 'Dolomite' Winter Olympic Games were held precisely here; and that the valley – surrounded by famous peaks, including Tofane, Cristallo, Faloria, Cinque Torri, Becco del Mezzodì, Sorapiss, and Croda da Lago – has been the setting for the high-altitude version of the Dolce Vita, and has always combined a passion for sport and worldly, stylish excess spiced with typical Italian vivacity. The myth of Cortina stars an 'old lady' (who has simply changed her makeup somewhat in order to appear younger and more beautiful): Hotel Cristallo, the first five-star luxury hotel in the Alps, which has spawned famous love stories and which served as the setting for cult movies, first and foremost *The Pink Panther* with Peter Sellers. The town boasts

132 - The pool at the Cristallo Hotel, the first 5-star luxury hotel in the Alps, opened in 1901.

133 - The symbol of Cortina is the 19th-century campanile of the Basilica of St. Philip and St. James, situated in the middle of this delightful town. The basilica is a favorite among those who want to celebrate a mountain wedding set against the backdrop of impressive Dolomite peaks.

a number of boutiques, restaurants, and night spots that would put many European capitals to shame. Furthermore, it has one of the largest areas for downhill and cross-country skiing in Europe, and, in its immediate vicinity, such natural phenomena as the Tre Cime di Lavaredo.

Cortina's coat of arms consists of a tower surrounded by two fir trees against a sky-blue background. Below these, on a gilt ribbon, appears the Latin motto *Modo vivo ac tuta quiesco,* or "I live frugally and sleep peacefully," which, let's admit it, could not be less appropriate for a place like the jewel of Ampezzano. But then again, besides being the Queen of the Dolomites, Cortina is also in Italy, a land of extraordinary beauty and twisted paradoxes.

134 / 135 - An icon of the alpine and tourist world; arguably, no peaks are more recognizable and photographed in the Dolomites than the three known as the Tre Cime di Lavaredo, which mark the boundary between the area of Ampezzano in the Veneto and Val Pusteria in Alto Adige. Also known as the 'three fingers of Dolomia,' these peaks blaze with incredible colors at sunset.

135 - A fantastic view of the Tofane, the most majestic massif in the eastern Dolomites. It boasts many famous ski runs as well as several climbing routes with cables, iron rungs, pegs, steps, etc. as well as extraordinary hiking trails.

Venice

Italy

What is seduction? Is it about seducing or being seduced? Or better, is it letting oneself be seduced, which presupposes an attitude both passive and active, fortuitous and intended? If you are in Venice, the last of these is most likely. You go there to let yourself be seduced, to indulge in the city's sheer beauty since it has always been an extraordinary setting for love... and the erotic. "Love keeps me alive only to allow me to die once again... Take my soul and give me yours," wrote Giacomo Casanova, the world-renowned prince of seducers, who, as he himself admitted, fell hopelessly in love time and time again, albeit for as little as one day.

So, are you in love, or do you hope to be? Don't waste a moinute: make plans for a getaway to Venice. In order to do things properly, go there in autumn, when this unique city is more romantic, sensitive, decadent, fragile, and evanescent than ever. And, let it be said, less besieged by tourists. In that season there is no need to worry about the fog rising from the lagoon (or about the possibility of floods). Nonetheless you must enjoy the obviously touristy experience of riding a gondola to admire the magnificent buildings and palaces

along the Grand Canal, pass under the Rialto Bridge, then penetrate the narrow, solitary canals, just as you must have a coffee at the legendary Caffé Florian on St. Mark's Square, which has been the elegant venue for romantic rendezvous since the age of Venetian courtesans, known as the 'geishas of the West.' The real problem with this city is deciding what to see because, leaving aside great architecture, there are so many artistic masterpieces in its churches, museums, and aristocratic mansions that it would take months to see them all, even if you limited your choice to the most famous sights such as St. Mark's Basilica, Santa Maria dei Miracoli, the Doge's Palace, the Museo Correr and the Ca' d'Oro.

Furthermore, nothing is quite as enjoyable as getting lost in Venice. It is inevitable in any case, especially if you walk around with a map in your hands. In short, you must let yourself be seduced – by the mad labyrinth of the city's alleys (*calli*) and small squares (*campielli*), by the handicraft workshops, and by the *bacari* – the traditional *osterias* in the neighborhoods known as Cannaregio and Dorsoduro, where the true soul of the Venetian

136 / 137 - The Rialto is the most famous of the four bridges that cross the Grand Canal. Without a doubt the most popular Venetian church is St. Mark's Basilica, with its Byzantine-style domes and tall Campanile dominating the square before it.

peop'e emerges. Another must is a ride on the waterbus or boats to visit the fascinating islands of the lagoon: Murano, the tiny capital of glass-blowing; Burano, the home of lacework; Giudecca, site of the Church of il Redentore designed by the great architect Palladio; and finally, 'rural' Torcello and the ethereal island of San Lazzaro degli Armeni, occupied by a mystic monastery.

As for lodgings, Venice offers a wide range of seductive cubbyholes and rooms with a view. But none can compare to the one on Riva degli Schiavoni, the historic Danieli Hotel that epitomizes Venice as the 'seductive Serenissima.' Overflowing with Byzantine-like velvet and gilding, it has witnessed the beginnings of innumerable great love affairs. One alone is enough to make our point – that between Alfred de Musset and George Sand, two emblematic figures of 19th-century literary Romanticism. He was 23 at and she was near'y 30 when their passionate affair was sparked by a note that de Musset sent to her at the Danieli Hotel: "My dear George, I have to tell you something stupid and ridiculous... I'm in love with you."

138 *top* - The gondola mooring before the Hotel Danieli on the Riva degli Schiavoni, which runs the entire length of the San Marco basin and is named after the merchants from Dalmatia, who were known as "Schiavonia" in the time of the Venetian Republic.

138 *bottom* - Everything is ready for dinner on the terrace of the Ristorante Terrazza Danieli at the Danieli Hotel. From here you have the same view as did Venetian noblemen, who once observed the arrival of ships loaded with goods from the Far East.

139 *top* - The oldest part of the Danieli is Palazzo Dandolo (with its fabulous hall and staircase), commissioned in the 14th century by the aristocratic Venetian family whose most famous forebear, Enrico Dandolo, took part in the sack of Constantinople and brought back fabulous booty of gold, marble and Byzantine objects.

139 *bottom* - It is impossible to calculate how many love stories began or were consummated at the seductive Danieli Hotel, but certainly the most famous of all was the one between George Sand and Alfred de Musset, who stayed in Room no. 10.

Verona

Italy

In a period when lovers send one another text messages, there is a girl in Verona who receives at least 4000 bona fide letters of this sort each year. Her name is Giulietta de' Capuleti (or Juliet), the heroine of the most beautiful and tragic love story of all time. Despite the fact that she is probably a fictitious creation of William Shakespeare (who never went to Verona), Juliet enjoys eternal life in this beautiful city and is a phenomenal tourist attraction. What is allegedly her home on Via Cappello, in the very heart of the old town, is a cult site for romantic souls all over the world. It is said that if you touch the right breast of her statue in the house's courtyard you will be lucky in love. Everyone loves to pose for a photograph in front of the famous balcony, even though it was actually added in a later

period to make for a more 'realistic' setting (the house dates to the 14th century). As for her tomb, located in the crypt of the former Capuchin convent, the sarcophagus is chipped away because visitors have been taking pieces of it as relics for centuries. Marie Louise of Austria, in fact, had some mounted on her jewelry. Each day people lay flowers and love letters before the tomb – which, by the way, is also a popular location for weddings. Indeed, there is a team of volunteers in Verona who take it upon themselves to answer all the letters, in various languages, signing them "Juliet's Secretary."

Leaving aside Shakespearian references, Verona truly deserves to be called the city of love. Surrounded by a bend in the Adige River, the old town could not be more romantic, especially

with such sights as the Piazza delle Erbe and Piazza Dante, which seem to have been laid out expressly for trysts; historic and architectural treasures, such as the Arena, one of the most fascinating Roman amphitheaters in Italy, which features a famous outdoor opera festival that attracts music lovers from all over the world; and the medieval Castelvecchio with its enchanting crenelated bridge over the river, which once served as the seat of power of the Scaligeri, the lords of the city. And, contradicting Shakespeare, who wrote that "there is no world outside Verona walls," the areas surroundings the city also offer fascinating sights that are an ode to the good life. All you need to do is travel a few miles outside the town to enjoy enchanting Lake Garda, or the lovely hilly region of Valpolicella with its

143 - Surrounded by an Italian garden, the elegant Villa Amistà, now the sophisticated Byblos Art Hotel, is situated in Valpolicella. The interiors are harmoniously characterized by a fine collection of contemporary art.

Portofino

Italy

144 - The characteristic small square in Portofino is the center of the world for this town's 500 citizens, as well as for the international jet set. Here a favorite among celebrities is the Belmond Hotel Splendido, located in a restored monastery that boasts an enchanting garden with centuries-old vegetation that cascades down towards the sea.

145 - Surrounded by pine and chestnut trees, amphitheater-shaped Portofino is protected by a regional nature reserve that extends for 8 miles along the coast.

Portofino is a small harbor opening out onto the sublime. Arriving here by sea in 1889, the great author Guy de Maupassant described it as a "small village that stretches in a crescent shape along a calm bay... Never have I experienced a sensation that can rival what I felt as I entered that cove;" and then again, "We make our way towards the amphitheater of the houses surrounded by intensely green, cool forests, all reflected in the mirror of calm water where some boats seem to be sleeping..." Were the author of *Bel-Ami* to go there now on a summer day, he might be even more amazed by the white forest created by the masts of the luxury yachts that vie for every last inch of the most popular and sought-after bay in Liguria.

Among high society the fortune and popularity of what in ancient Roman times was known as *Portus Delphini* – after its dolphins, which to this day leap and dance in this sea in an area now a national park – began even before the French author's ecstatic reaction as quoted above. Already in 1845 the British consul in Genoa purchased the fort of Portofino from the Kingdom of Sardinia and made it his summer residence. He was followed by many aristocrats from all over Europe, who had splendid villas built right behind the village or, in a later period, chose to stay at the elegant Belmond Hotel Splendido during their vacations. This hotel, a restored old monastery, is a must for those who want to discover Portofino (as well as

the other treasures of the Ligurian coast). With a garden situated on a steep hill and a triumph of bougainvillea, palm trees and centuries-old olive trees, it demonstrates how already early on this entire area achieved a harmonious relationship between man and nature. You can also stay at Belmond Splendido Mare located in the famous Piazzetta.

Indeed, the stretch of coastline by Portofino boasts a great number of extraordinary examples of cultural activity. A short boat trip will take you to San Fruttuoso, the tiny bay dominated by a mystical Benedictine abbey of the same name, the dome of which emerges as if by magic from the thick Mediterranean maquis brushwood. Further on but nearby is Cinque Terre, a cluster of five picturesque and colorful villages – Monterosso, Vernazza, Corniglia, Manarola, and Riomaggiore – that rise vertically from the cliff, as if challenging the law of gravity. Surrounded by vineyards and olive tree terraces alternating with forests and lovely white pebble coves, these villages are interconnected by a path famous for being the world's most fascinating coastal hike. Although you must be in tip-top shape to walk the entire Cinque Terre, a stretch of land that almost anyone can negotiate lies between Manarola and Riomaggiore. About 1100 yards long, it winds above the sea through what can solely be described as romantic scenery. And, in fact, it is called Via dell'Amore or Love Way.

146 - In a spectacular position on a precipitous cliff, Manarola is connected to the village of Riomaggiore by a path with panoramic views that runs among the rocks and is known as Via dell'Amore or Love Way.

147 *top* - The tower of Castle of the Doria dominates the promontory of Vernazza, the second of the famous maritime villages of Cinque Terre.

147 *bottom* - On the coast of Monterosso, the bronze statue of St. Francis caressing his faithful German Shepherd seems spellbound by the enchanting beauty of the area of Cinque Terre.

Côte d'Azur

France

The person who coined the name 'Côte d'Azur' for this coastline – the area extending from Genoa to Marseilles, but especially the part between Menton and St Raphaël, was the Burgundian author and poet Stephen Liégeard. That was in 1887. Liégeard was basically broad-minded and intelligent, but he could never have imagined that his metaphor would become not only a geographical marker, but also a sort of trademark, recognized and used all over the world. Indeed the raison d'être of the Côte d'Azur appears to be the principle of serving Beauty, with a capital 'B.'

Its light is unparalleled, nearly insolent, as are its colors and scents, those of the sea and flowers. Every locality here has its own story and appeal, from Monte Carlo with its somewhat kitsch extravagance to Antibes and Cap Ferrat, the exclusive 'millionaires' peninsula,' from Nice and its air of grandeur, to Cannes and Saint-Tropez, magnificent towns known for their scintillating, fashionable atmosphere. These are but the most famous of the gems along the Côte d'Azur, which has so many other marvelous sights

in store for visitors in its immediate surroundings, known as the arriére-pays or interior: a long, simply unforgettable succession of villages perchés, hamlets and villages perched on rocky spurs whose architecture blends perfectly with the romantic, lush scenery. And it is not by coincidence that these same villages have, like honey, attracted a host of artists, and that each of them has left his mark. Haut-de-Cagnes, lying on a hill near Nice, was the getaway of the painter Auguste Renoir (his home is now a fine museum). The stairs bordered by bougainvillaea in Biot inspired the fantastic works of Fernand Léger, who left behind a huge, dazzling mosaic. At Èze, a delightful 'eagle's nest' inside Monaco, house facades are adorned with quotes from the philosopher Nietzsche, who wrote part of Thus Spake Zarathustra here. The town of Vence boasts the Chapelle du Rosaire, better known as the Matisse Chapel after the great artist who designed and decorated this gift, which he considered his masterpiece, for the Côte d'Azur – a work in which the area's archetypical colors seem to have a life of their own.

148 / 149 - Guests enjoy the sun at the pool of the legendary Colombe d'Or hotel while admiring a huge installation by Alexander Calder. The famous hotel lies in the charming hillside village of St -Paul-de-Vence, a favorite among great artists such as Picasso and Matisse.

And only a few miles away is the most famous village, Saint-Paul-de-Vence, whose atmosphere is imbued with art. Among its more than 100 galleries, the most prestigious is an inn that has been turned into a legendary hotel, La Colombe d'Or, which for decades has belonged to the Roux family. The primogenitor had the foresight to ask his clients to pay him with works of art. Consequently the hotel rooms, built atop a series of enchanting terraces overflowing with flowers, all have paintings, drawings, collages, sculptures, photographs and memorabilia by artists such as Picasso, Chagall, Miró, Dubuffet, Soutine, Modigliani and Calder.

150 - A view of the Vieux Port or old harbor of Cannes, a town that is one of the eternal myths of the Côte d'Azur. Not far away are the delightful Marché aux Fleurs (flower market) and legendary Croisette promenade.

151 *top* - It was no accident that Francis Scott Fitzgerald set his famous novel *Tender Is the Night* in Antibes, a splendid town on the cape of the same name that is dominated by the star-shaped Fort Carré, which affords panoramic views of the region.

151 *bottom* - The light of the sunset creates warm colors that bathe the facades of the houses along the marina of Saint-Tropez, which is always full of celebrities and luxury yachts – as well as the usual group of paparazzi – from May to September.

The Tuscan Hills
Italy

152 - The dome of the Basilica of Santa Maria del Fiore, a masterpiece designed by Brunelleschi, dominates the enchanting panorama of Florence.

152 *bottom and* 153 - In a region of such divine beauty as Tuscany, perhaps the best perspective, so to speak, is to be had from the sky. In this way one can admire the characteristic shell-like shape of the famous Piazza del Campo in Siena, the venue of the equestrian Palio, as well as the striking towers of the equally marvelous town of San Gimignano, which lie behind the town's nickname: 'Manhattan of the Middle Ages.'

The papal suite is a triumph of purple and yellow velvet with a Renaissance bed large enough for four persons. The Napoleonic suite is decorated with a collection of 100 busts and statuettes of the emperor, while the majolica suite has a showcase with a precious wedding kimono that was given to the first Duke of Genoa by the Empress of Japan. They say that the curators at the Metropolitan Museum of Art in New York would give anything to obtain the furnishings in La Suvera, the medieval fortress in the vicinity of Siena that Pope Julius II converted into a Renaissance pleasure villa in 1507. Now the property of the Marquis Ricci, this veritable jewel – which boasts numerous works of art, a museum protected by UNESCO, and an equally spectacular Italian garden – is on the top ten list of the most luxurious and fascinating relais in Tuscany.

For that matter, one must stay in such a place to experience to the utmost a region like Tuscany, of which every square yard has been depicted in a painting, sung in an opera, or used as the setting for a novel or movie. This is the incomparable allure of the most Italian region in Italy. In a certain sense, Tuscany belongs to each of us, even those who come from afar. While admiring the soft hills, the ridges at sunset, the vineyards and rows of cypress trees, you

have the sensation of looking at a masterpiece of nature and man – both of which have worked side by side for centuries – perhaps more than in any other part of the world – to reveal its absolute beauty. The treasures of Florence, for example, are too numerous to include in an itinerary of this Renaissance capital, yet they cannot be divorced from the landscape, both natural and cultural, of the Arno River and the amphitheater of hills that surrounds the city, including its gardens, from the famous Boboli to the romantic rose garden that descends toward the city from Piazzale Michelangelo. And not even Siena – with its world-famous Piazza del Campo and Cathedral, that bicolored gem with so many esoteric symbols – would be the same without its exceptional and spectacular position overlooking the surrounding countryside.

The best way to explore the environs of Florence is on a mountain bike along the unpaved, winding roads – a heritage protected from the onslaughts of modernity – that constitute the so-called Anello del Rinascimento or Renaissance Ring, a long itinerary of an almost perfect circular shape, the hub of which is Brunelleschi's dome atop Florence Cathedral. The road runs from Fiesole to the region of Chianti through countryside dotted with beautiful parish

154 - Vineyards, olive and cypress trees, old houses and dirt roads that seem to fade away into oblivion: landscape becomes a sublime art in the Tuscan hills.

155 - Situated a short distance from Siena is the Relais La Suvera, a dream hotel in the middle of a romantic Italian-style garden. Originally a medieval fortress, it was converted by Pope Julius II into a Renaissance pleasure villa in the early 16th century.

churches, castles, and villages. As for the area around Siena, if possible it is even richer in attractions, with such astounding sights as San Gimignano, 'the city of a Hundred Towers' between the regions of Chianti and Val d'Elsa. Then again, there is Val d'Orcia with the towns of Montepulciano and Montalcino, both of which are world-famous for their great wines, among other things, and Bagno Vignoni, a romantic hamlet and spa that has been everyone's favorite since the time of the Etruscans. A list of the marvels in Tuscany would continue forever because, though they are all 'too well-known,' the hills of this magical land reward you with sensations that go straight to the heart.

The Amalfi Coast
Italy

156 - 1197 feet above sea level, Ravello is the astounding balcony overlooking the Amalfi coast. It was 'discovered' and frequented by leading personalities in the world of art and culture, and hosts a prestigious festival dedicated to Richard Wagner each summer.

157 - The light kindles the facades of the houses in this splendid view of the old village of Praiano, the pride and joy of which is the Marina di Praia, the only beach on the Amalfi coast that catches the sun until evening.

After a debate that lasted an entire summer, the men in Positano all agreed that a woman's breasts are either beautiful or ugly, and that's that. Therefore, they have to be covered. This was the summer of 1959, when Positano (which had already had a peek of the first topless swimsuits, albeit hidden behind cliffs) imported the bikini fashion to Italy. While the men argued, their women were busy crocheting the two tiny pieces of this new item that was to become the rage among female tourists. And, while they were at it, they also set about sewing beach robes from the hemp that they normally used for kitchen towels. This marked the birth of the 'Positano style' – comfortable, colorful, and shabby, hence, terribly chic – which has never been out of fashion henceforth. A summer classic, it is to fashion what the Doric style is to architecture.

The same holds true for Positano as a whole. While this picturesque village is the liveliest and most sophisticated place on the Amalfi Coast – as well as the closest to those arriving from Naples – the entire coastline in the region of Campania has always been on top of the list of wished-for romantic vacations, and is also highly epicurean.

But it must be said that the Amalfi Coast has to be earned. Despite its stunningly beautiful views of enchanting coves, rugged terrain with vineyards and lemon trees, picture-postcard hamlets with the

fragrance of flowers (as well as fried tidbits and tomato sauce), and the sound of languid Neapolitan songs, these 30 miles or so of winding road are the nightmare of every motorist. And, when you finally manage somehow to park your car, you have to deal with maddening vertical town planning. As the famous author John Steinbeck wrote in his article on Positano in *Harper's Bazaar*, "You do not walk to see a friend, you either climb or slide." But how wonderful it is to slide into this sea, or enjoy the miracle of Amalfi, the delightful 'capital' that boasts a long and glorious maritime history! Not to mention Furore, the traditional hamlet no larger than a condominium. Again, by proceeding southward, you come across Cetara, famous for its savory filtered anchovy sauce, a favorite with the ancient Romans, unbeatable with spaghetti, and Vietri sul Mare, the home of multicolored pottery.

Finally, a small detour from the main road, on a level with Maiori and Minori, winds its way up the Valle del Dragone to Ravello, the splendid balcony of the Amalfi Coast. With its small churches and the Villa Rufolo, considered a 'minor Alhambra' because of its mixture of architectural styles – from ancient Roman to medieval – along with a garden of palm and fruit trees and bougainvillaea, and which in July and August is the venue of a prestigious music festival, Ravello is *the* romantic destination of the entire coast and has

been so since the time of the Grand Tour. It was visited by Goethe, Wagner, Giuseppe Verdi, André Gide, D.H. Lawrence, Virginia Woolf, Greta Garbo, and Federico Fellini – all of whom fell in love with it. And, it goes without saying, Ravello has the highest concentration of luxury hotels along the coastline, favorites with honeymooners. One of these is the super-luxurious Belmond Hotel Caruso, set in a converted 11th-century mansion that boasts a unique position between the sky and sea.

158 / 159 - The infinity pool of the Belmond Hotel Caruso in Ravello is a masterpiece of contemporary architecture that offers wonderful panoramic views. Another treasure here is the 11th-century building that houses this splendid hotel, a favorite among authors such as Virginia Woolf, Graham Greene, and Gore Vidal.

Korčula
Croatia

In Italy some people were angry to learn that during his official visit to Beijing, Stipe Mesić, the first president of independent Croatia, boasted about a centuries-old connection between China and the small island town on the eastern coast of the Adriatic thanks to the adventurous travels of an illustrious fellow citizen of Croatia, Marco Polo. Attributing Croatian citizenship to the author of *The Travels of Marco Polo* is pure exaggeration, to say the least. Yet it is true that some documents state that Marco Polo was born in 1254 on the island of Korčula, which, at the time, was one of the jewels of the Venetian Republic.

On Korčula, more precisely in the charming town the island is named after (a kind of miniature Venice, with similar atmosphere and architecture, as well as an impressive cathedral dedicated to St. Mark and decorated with paintings by Tiepolo and Tintoretto), the locals have made Marco Polo a tourist attraction; what may be the house in which he was born has been converted into an imaginative museum on his adventures. In the summer, on the other hand, before the gate in the old city wall, there are daily performances of the *Moreška*, the

old war dance used to ward off the attacks of the Turks, who were always attracted to the treasures kept on the island. On top of all this, Korčula has recently been placed on the list of the 100 most romantic places in the world thanks to the opening of a luxury hotel, the Lešić Dimitri Palace, which occupies the majestic former bishop's palace in the medieval heart of the town. Six elegant residences are reserved for guests, each with furnishings that reflect the style of the various stages of the Silk Road followed by Marco Polo. The hotel includes a restaurant and a classy spa.

Even at the height of the summer season, the island – which is nearly 31 miles long and 4.3 miles at its widest point – offers many interesting places far from the massive tourist attractions. Along the coastline are magnificent bays with white sand (such as Lumbarda, deservedly the most famous) and rock ledges that slope down towards a fantastic aquamarine sea. But you should not overlook the villages – both along the seaside and in the countryside – and the scenery on the interior of the island, where terraced vineyards alternate with pine forests and stretches of scrubland.

160 / 161 - Breakfast on the terrace overlooking the sea in one of the exclusive residences of Lešić Dimitri Palace in Korčula, the town on the island of the same name in southern Dalmatia that is famous for being the birthplace of Marco Polo, as well as for its typically Venetian architecture.

In addition, the town of Korčula is separated from the mainland by a strait less than half a mile wide and on the level of Orebić, another historic maritime site and the most important town on Pelješac, the largest peninsula along the Adriatic after Istria. Shaped like a finger pointing to the sea, Pelješac is ideal for hikers and gourmets. The former can walk along the paved path laid out by Napoleonic troops when the French emperor ruled over the provinces of Illyria, while the latter can visit the beautiful fortified hamlet of Ston and spend the evening at an inn facing the sea to taste, by candlelight, the famous, aphrodisiac oysters that are cultivated here.

Santorini
Greece

162 - Clinging to the rocks of the spectacular caldera of Santorini, Oia is the most picturesque village on this island, a fascinating combination of rock-hewn whitewashed houses (some of which have become chic shops and art galleries), churches with turquoise domes, narrow staircases, and fragrant flowers. Here you must not miss the most famous and 'fiery' sunset in the entire Mediterranean.

163 - The magnificent infinity pool at the Mystique Resort, whose name already promises guests a super-romantic vacation that is both sensual and spiritual.

Called Kallisté – "the most beautiful" – by the ancients, this island emerges from the Aegean Sea like a pincer surrounding the caldera of an underwater volcano formed by an apocalyptic eruption that took place sometime around 1560 BC. According to archeologists, this was the same eruption that marked the birth of the legendary island of Atlantis, which later disappeared into the sea. Santorini is thus a mythical island with a mythical landscape consisting of 984-foot-high black lava cliffs and beaches like Perissa and Kamari with iron-gray or – in the case of the splendid Kokkini Ammos, purple sand. Thirasía, Palea Kameni and Nea Kameni, the tiny volcanic islands in the caldera, still exude sulfuric vapor and contain hot geothermal springs.

Santorini is certainly not comfortable. Today, as people did 1000 years ago, you go to the beach on a donkey because only this tenacious animal (so highly regarded that it enjoys special status here) is able to go up and down the dizzying paths of this island. Women who insist on wearing high-heel shoes do so at their own risk because the towns of Thira and Oia are laid out vertically, with a labyrinth of stairs and steps, as if challenging the law of gravity. In short, what you need here is a good dose of stamina and resistance to heat, which is merciless in summer. Or better, a romantic and contemplative character, because Santorini reveals all its dramatic beauty when the sun sinks into the caldera during a fiery sunset, creating a breathtaking spectacle of picturesque cubic architecture tinged with orange and violet. An Anglo-Hellenic word, *Sunsetarides*, has even been coined for the tourists who

reserve a seat each afternoon to enjoy the best view – paying a pretty penny for the privilege – in the first row of the terraces of the cafés overlooking the caldera. But it is precisely because of these sunsets, the small whitewashed houses, and the turquoise-domed churches, that Santorini is considered one of the most romantic islands in the world, as well as a favorite location for honeymoons and weddings. Four thousand of the latter are celebrated each year from May to October; each local hotel even has its own wedding planning agency that organizes civil or religious ceremonies along the seaside, on a terrace overlooking the blue Aegean, or in special locations such as vineyards perched on the rocks of the archeological site of Akrotiri, the island's Pompeii, or before the monastery of Profitis Ilias near the village of Pyrgos, on the highest point of Santorini, where on a clear day you can see as far as the distant island of Crete. And every hotel competes with the rest when it comes to creating a dream-like atmosphere, with scented gardens, leisure-inviting spas and white suites that combine ethnic Mediterranean style with ultramodern design, each with its own balcony framed by the sea and sky. Our favorite resort lies in the village of Oia, and even its name, Mystique, promises (and actually delivers) an ultra-romantic vacation. You can choose from among suites called Vibrant, Allure, or Spiritual, and enjoy a privileged position and view of the sunset from the Aura bar. And in the evening you can dine under the stars at the Charisma restaurant or in a cool cellar with a vaulted ceiling known as Secret, amid a triumph of candles and passionate red roses.

Andalusia
Spain

164 *top* - A spectacular works of Moorish Revival architecture, Seville's semicircular Plaza de España embodies the strong bond between the mother country and its American colonies.

164 *bottom* - The entrance to the marvelous and exotic Hotel Alfonso XIII, opened in 1929 on the occasion of the Ibero-American Exposition of Seville.

165 - One of the most fascinating parts of the Alhambra in Granada is the Patio de los Arrayanes, or Court of the Myrtle, so named for the myrtle bushes that border the sides of the pool. A masterpiece of Moorish-Andalusian art and architecture, this building complex stands from a hill with the Sierra Nevada Mountains as a backdrop.

Carmen and Don Juan. She is the symbol of unbridled sensuality, the wild gypsy, the irresistible and eternal personification of the feminine. He is the prince of seducers, who, according to legend 'conquered' 1003 women in Spain and several hundred others elsewhere in Europe, the quintessence of Eros as a magnificent lie. She was created by the pen of Mérimée and the music of Bizet, while he was immortalized by Mozart. It is certainly no accident that both hail from Andalusia, the land that seems to live and feed on strong emotions. Other 'Andalusians' include flamenco, a dance form that is the very embodiment of passion; the mythical matador, who inflames spectators in the bullring during the elegant and cruel spectacle of *sangre y arena* (blood and sand); and the most fervid (and passionate) *Semana Santa* or Easter Week in Catholic Spain.

The Moors, who ruled Andalusia for a few centuries before the 'Reconquest' by Christians in 1492 – and who reconciled science and magic despite being great mathematicians and astronomers – called it *Jezira al-Andalus*, the Island of Andalusia. And in a certain sense they marked the destiny of this region. To this day Andalusia is an island, which, though part of the mainland, is neither in Europe or Africa, but is simply itself, with all the intriguing allure and languid, sweet pleasure of a distant land.

The sights in Andalusia and the sensations they elicit cannot all be listed here. There is, for example, the Alhambra in Granada, one of the supreme gems of Islamic art whose elaborate stonework stands out against the white background of the Sierra Nevada range. Next, by following the scents of the orange trees that line all the streets in the historic center of Cordoba, you will arrive at the Mezquita, the superb mosque with, an opulent Baroque cathedral inside that stands in striking contrast to the ethereal geometric patterns of the Islamic structure. Andalusia is reflected in the vast spaces and bright colors of the Costa de la Luz and plains around Jerez de la Frontera, the land of the wildest horses and most inebriating wine, sherry. Or it reveals itself gradually in the myriad white villages nestling in the valley of the Guadalquivir, the river that crosses through Andalusia, which is also the land of the contagious gaiety of the *bodegas* (wine shops and cellars) and of the romantic intimacy of patios, which, decorated with flowers, were designed by Muslim architects as images of earthly paradise.

However, the heart of Andalusian enchantment and passion lies in Seville, the southernmost and most exotic large city in Europe, which, with its incredible Islamic and Christian architecture and ubiquitous exciting scent of flowers, is the ideal setting for a love story. To experience all its passions you must indulge in the pleasure of spending a night in one of the romantic rooms in the marvelous Alfonso XIII Hotel, founded in 1929 as the most exotic grand hotel in Europe. Its name is a tribute to the king of Spain at the time, but its charm is that of Carmen and Don Juan.

The Douro Valley

Portugal

166 - A detail of the façade of the Casa Mateus, considered the best example of Baroque architecture in Portugal. Built in the first half of the 18th century, and attributed to the Italian architect Nicola Nasoni, this palace is situated in the town of Vila Real and is one of the jewels of the Douro Valley, together with the splendid old wineries that produce the noble wine known as Port in this area.

167 - A view of Ribeira, the most picturesque quarter in the city of Porto, connected to the municipality of Vila Nova de Gaia by a bridge over the Douro River that was designed by a student of Gustave Eiffel.

When it opened in 1886 (constructed to a design by a student of Gustave Eiffel), the Dom Luís Bridge was the longest iron arch bridge ever built. But even now that it no longer holds this record, the 'horizontal Eiffel Tower' spanning the Douro River and connecting the cities of Porto and Vila Nova de Gaia is still a masterpiece of engineering and elegance. Indeed, no work could be more suitable as the gateway to the Douro Valley, the land of famous Port wine. Situated on terraces hewn out of rock on terrain dotted with granite peaks, the vineyards extend for 250,000 hectares, creating one of the most spectacular rural landscapes ever fashioned by man, an area placed on the UNESCO World Heritage List.

Except for the three winter months – and at the high point of September, during the grape harvest – the Douro Valley is an unforgettable venue for an epicurean and romantic vacation. While an automobile is the most obvious means of getting around and discovering the wineries, all of which are open for visits and wine-tasting, it is really worthwhile making a tour along the river on a *barco rabelo*, a traditional cargo boat used as long ago as the 17th century to transport wine barrels but now used for pleasure cruises. A delightful alternative is to travel along the valley on the historic steam train and discover the joy of moving slowly (the speed never exceeds 18 mph) on a railway line that

passes through 26 tunnels and over 30 bridges and formidable landscapes, and which allows passengers to see the most beautiful stations in Portugal, from the first, the São Bento station in Porto, to those at Régua and Pinhão, which are literally carpeted with azulejo tiles. Régua also deserves a visit: the Museu do Douro or Douro Museum and the Vila Real, which has the Casa Mateus, the most beautiful Baroque estate in the country, surrounded by an Italianate garden and vineyards that produce a famous rosé. At Pinhão, on the other hand, you must take your time to indulge in a *tour de force* among the famous estates, from Croft's Quinta da Roeda to Graham's Quinta dos Malvedos. Among the other villages in the valley are enchanting Sabrosa, where the famous navigator and explore Ferdinand Magellan was born in 1480, and Lamego, which boasts many monuments, including the medieval Chapel of São Pedro de Balsemão, Portugal's oldest church, and the Sanctuary of Our Lady of the Remedies, which dominates the town from atop a hill: here on September 8 takes place a splendidly colorful pilgrimage that also marks the beginning of the grape harvest. Finally, there is the Aquapura, a dream hotel in a 19th-century aristocratic building. Among its many marvels is a swimming pool overlooking the river and a fantastic spa, where you can be pampered with – what else? – grape-based massages.

The Azores
Portugal

According to legend, the Azores, which lie almost halfway between Portugal and North America, are the remains of the mythical continent of Atlantis. There is some scientific proof for this theory. The islands constitute the most recently formed land on earth, the result of intense volcanic activity that is still evident: the soft, dark sand of the beaches; the streams of petrified lava of the spectacular rock formations; the small, still geo-thermally active crater lakes; and the perfect cone of the 7713-foot volcano that dominates the island of Pico, the highest peak in Portugal as well as an ideal site for trekking.

However, do not expect the nine islands of this archipelago to be a wild, barren microcosm inhabited by those primitive people who, from the early 17th century until about 30 years ago, engaged in ferocious whale hunting. Surprisingly, there are fewer 'sea dogs' (now used as expert guides for watching whales, which are at home in the waters of the Azores) than farmers here because the fertile volcanic soil and mild climate have made the islands a veritable garden in the middle of the ocean.

Orange orchards lie side by side with vineyards, and pastures of a dazzling green dotted with cow herds create a countryside that looks like an exotic and incongruous Swiss landscape. Moreover, each island has its own character. São Miguel, the largest and most 'international,' is home to the delightful capital of the archipelago, Ponta Delgada. Faial, an obligatory stopping point for Atlantic crossings, is the most maritime. Santa Maria is known for its sweet Mediterranean quality, Graciosa is famous for its vineyards and windmills, and Terceira has a historic atmosphere as well as the town of Angra, founded in the 15th century, which boasts splendid architecture decorated with azulejos tiles. And while Pico, São Jorge and Corvo offer enchanting scenery with mountains and dramatic, steep cliffs that plunge into the blue sea, the most romantic island is certainly Flores, the western-most point of Europe, whose name ('flowers') is due to the carpet of blue and pink hydrangeas that, though quite common in the entire archipelago, here grow into incredibly large and tall bushes, tenderly embracing every village and lining small country roads – including

168 / 169 - The island of Flores is the westernmost strip of land of the Azores and, indeed, of the European continent. It is a fantastic combination of idyllic beaches, deep valleys, rugged peaks, hot springs, and waterfalls. The most spectacular of these falls is the Ribeira Grande, in the vicinity of the town of Fajazinha, which actually consists of at least 20 falls, some of which plunge into the ocean.

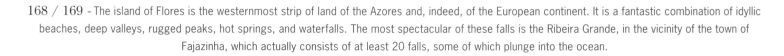

the one that leads to the Aldeia da Cuada, an old estate whose buildings are made of dark stone and have been converted into the most fascinating rural tourist structure in the archipelago. A vacation here means marvelous days surrounded by green and blue, long walks in the lush countryside, and an enjoyable swim in the ocean or the turquoise lagoons of the caldera. And unforgettable nights in the dream-like atmosphere of the 'end of the (old) world.'

170 / 171 - Flores owes its name to the profusion of flowers that embellish its valleys. Huge hortensia bushes with pink or blue petals can be seen everywhere, bordering the pastures, vineyards, and wheat fields.

171 - One of the green valleys in Flores is home to rustic Aldeia da Cuada, the most fascinating farm holiday complex in the Azores.

Marrakech

Morocco

172 *top and* 173 - In the evening, Jemaa-el-Fnaa Square is the venue of an extraordinary spectacle – one that has not changed since time immemorial – that of a multitude of vendors of food, orange juice and all sorts of wares, snake charmers and dancers, magicians, storytellers, and fortune tellers. All these can be viewed from the café terraces though it's better to take an active part in this colorful and chaotic scene.

172 *bottom* - The intoxicating fragrance of the plants, fig trees, and oleanders wafts through the garden as the babbling fountains enhance the balmy atmosphere of the magical Ksar Char-Bagh, a Moorish palace in the palm orchard of Marrakesh, that has now been converted into a luxury hotel.

On any morning at the Café de la Poste, the chatter of the habitués s much more delectable to those interested in the latest gossip than are the mint tea or date and honey sweets. It doesn't take much effort to link the given names, uttered with nonchalance, to the family names of international celebrities who have made Marrakesh their vacation home. That is the way things are nowadays. Although UNESCO wanted to protect them as Masterpieces of the Oral and Intangible Heritage of Humanity, the voices of Marrakesh are no longer those of the storytellers of the square and marketplace of Jemaa-el-Fnaa, nor even those of the alley ways registered half a century ago by author Elias Canetti in his formidable travel diary. The legendary and always marvelous square was recently renovated but must now be content with its role as 'costar' in the huge 'living room' that is the most seductive and captivating in Morocco. Nowadays people gather in other places, from the super chic restaurants situated in the old houses of the Medina – like the one in the sumptuous *riad* that once belonged to the French stylist Pierre Balmain – where gourmets luxuriate in the choice and 'acrobatic' *nouvelle cuisine marocaine*, to contemporary art and ethnic fashion galleries that by now are more numerous than traditional shops in this colorful souk, or in the heconistic 'foreigners-only' hammams, where you can spend the entire afternoon alternating between steam and rosewater baths. Above all, the *riad* in the historic quarters and the *ksour* or fortified villages nestled in the vast palm grove on the outskirts of the

city have all been transformed into hotels that feature fabulous rooms and areas for refined aesthetes, the walls of which are painted in the *tadelakt* technique (a word that derives from the Arabic verb 'to caress') and whose furnishings combine an ethnic style with state-of-the-art design. Among these, mention must be made of a terrestrial paradise, the Ksar Char-Bagh resort, considered one of the chicest hotels in the world.

In short, the mythical Ville Rouge or Red City is now worlds apart from the 'authentic' Morocco, but at the same time it is a perfect representation of what the collective imagination identifies as *the* place for an exotic, dream-like vacation. Besides such historic monuments as the Ben Youssef Madrasa, the tombs of the Saadi dynasty and the Badi Palace, the present-day list of sights to visit includes the Majorelle Garden (in the Nouvelle Ville) surrounding the villa (now the Islamic Art Museum), which for years was the refuge and source of inspiration for Yves Saint-Laurent. The great *couturier* purchased it from the heirs of Jacques Majorelle, the first European painter to be hypnotized by the fascination of Marrakesh in the 1920s and who immortalized its incredible colors on his canvases, inventing even new ones, such as the blue he used for the walls of local houses. Made even more vivid by the African sun, this is a truly magical color, one that does not exist in nature. But it is perhaps the best symbol of Marrakesh, the city that allows all people to transform their dreams into reality. For a lifetime or only for a weekend.

Along the Nile

Egypt

174 - On the east bank of the Nile, the gigantic temple complex of Luxor is one of the treasures of the ancient city of Thebes, dedicated to the god Amon. Construction on it began in the 14th century BC, but the period of greatest expansion occurred a century later, during the reign of the Pharaoh Ramesses II. On the west bank of the river is the City of the Dead, with the funerary temple of Queen Hatshepsut, one of the most extraordinary Egyptian monuments of antiquity.

175 - A splendid, panoramic aerial view of the remarkable archeological ruins of Elephantine Island, situated opposite the town of Aswan.

What do the great author Gustave Flaubert, the queen of mystery stories Agatha Christie, the adventurer Lawrence of Arabia and Florence Nightingale, the most famous nurse in history, have in common? They have all shared – albeit not together, of course – the experience of a cruise on the Nile River aboard a *dahabiya*, the traditional flat keeled sailing boat that dates back to the time of the Egyptian pharaohs. Those were the good old days, you might be tempted to say, ones that have apparently survived in our memory thanks only to engravings and old sepia-toned photographs, and at the dawn of tourism, when the Grand Tour among the treasures of ancient Egypt was still a luxury only for the privileged few. For that matter, as early as 1909, when he wrote his guidebook to Egypt, the French author and tireless globetrotter Pierre Loti already complained about the infernal noise made by the motors of 'modern' tourist vessels, which in his opinion had spoiled the allure of the "immense sanctuary" of Luxor. No offense intended to Loti, but to this day the trip on the Nile is – despite its popularity – a grand experience, the protagonists of which are the magnificent monuments of ancient Egyptian civilization. 'Touristic' Luxor (which should be visited in a gig along with a stop for a drink in one of the hotels, constructed during the time of the British Governorate and thus dignified by history) is surpassed by the grandiosity of ancient Thebes, capital of the dynasties of the New Kingdom (1570-1070 BC). Here it is absolutely thrilling to visit the 'city of the living' along an avenue lined with sculptures of sphinxes that connects the temples of Luxor and Karnak, and – beyond the river – the 'city of the dead,' with the pharaonic tombs in the Valley of the Kings and the Valley of the Queens, the Colossi of Memnon, and the frescoes in the Temple of Hatshepsut.

Then, as a special surprise – thanks to a small, exclusive tour operator, Nour el Nil – you can still take a cruise on the Nile 'à la Flaubert,' that is, on a 19th-century *dahabiya*, a romantic dream come true that lasts six days and five nights, during which you will stop at Esna, the locale renowned for the magnificent Temple of Khnum that lies about 25 miles south of Luxor and reach the final destination at Aswan, near the extraordinary monuments of the ancient kingdom of Nubia. Along the way you can stop not only at famous archeological sites – from the temple of Nekhbet to one dedicated to Horus at Edfu, and from the Sanctuary of Horemheb to the Ptolemaic temple of Kom Ombo – but also at river villages that are still off the beaten mass-tourist path in order to drink tea in a palm grove or venture on foot into the canyons that lead to the sands of the Sahara Desert.

Each *dahabiya* can hold at most 20 passengers, two in each of the cabins, which afford wonderful views and are furnished like alcoves in the *Thousand and One Nights*. The boat also has a large deck where you can lie in the sun and let yourself be pampered by the attentive and discreet staff on board, and where you can enjoy the beauty of the eternal scenery of the oldest river in the world.

176 *top* - Of all the vessels cruising down the Nile, the *dahabiya* is the only one to do so with sails, and thus offers a silent dream-like voyage much like the one enjoyed in the past by figures such as Flaubert and Lawrence of Arabia.

176 *bottom* - Two of the walls (and the furniture) are white, while the rest have two large windows that afford views of the Nile River landscape; waking up in one of the magnificent suites of a *dahabiya* is an unforgettable experience.

177 *top* - The elegant living room of a Nour et Nil Co. *dahabiya*, in which everything down to the tiniest detail is perfect.

177 *bottom* - You can sunbathe on the *dahabiya*, enjoy the river breeze, and dine while admiring the fabulous scenery along the banks of the Nile – ancient temples, quaint villages, farmland, and expanses of papyrus plants – on a slow and relaxing 6-day voyage from Luxor to Aswan that you will wish could last forever.

Seychelles

Republic of Seychelles

178 - Voted one of the ten most beautiful beaches in the world, Anse Victorin is a masterpiece of nature on Frégate Island. Thirty-four miles east of Mahé, this island, with a surface area of little more than 0.77 square miles, is lined with 7 magnificent beaches and thick forests with takamaka, cashew and Indian almond trees. It is also the home to around 2000 Aldabra giant tortoises – the emblematic animal of the Seychelles – which move around freely here.

179 - Frégate Island has 17 exclusive residences built of granite masses that dominate the beaches and have private swimming pools.

The *coco de mer* or sea coconut is the largest fruit. It can weigh as much as 44 pounds and is suggestively similar to a woman's pelvis. On the other hand, the inflorescence of its palm tree has a manifestly masculine aspect. According to Creole hearsay, sea coconut palms mate only during stormy nights, and it takes ten years for the fruit of their union to mature. Whether or not you believe in the possibility of seeing 'plant coitus,' sea coconut palms are an oddity of nature that can be admired in that Garden of Eden that goes under the name of Vallée de Mai, which, together with the enchanting beaches of Anse Lazio and Anse Georgette, are the treasures of Praslin, the second largest island of the Seychelles.

But the entire archipelago is a phenomenal sampling of natural marvels, beginning with its division between Inner and Outer Islands. The former group numbers 43, which are predominantly granitic, including the three largest – Mahé, Praslin and La Digue – where most of the population and the tourist structures of this republic are concentrated. There are 72 Outer Islands, coralline jewels scattered like coriander in the Indian Ocean, 13 of which take the shape of a crown around Aldabra, the largest atoll in the world. And while it is obvious that the subaquatic life here is extraordinary, the land is equally a living museum of natural history as well as a sanctuary for some of the rarest flora and fauna species on earth. The flora include the prehistoric and tentacular jellyfish tree, only 8 populations of which still survive,

and sensual orchids, while the fauna comprises a huge number of birds and the world's largest population of giant tortoises. With great foresight, about half of the archipelago has been declared a reserve. Furthermore, the respect for nature here is equal to that for local culture, a mixture of African, Madagascan, and European influences that is particularly evident in music and dance, especially the *moutya* dance, with its distinctly erotic character.

It would be a pity to consider the Seychelles as merely a series of beaches. Depending on the season, all of which are influenced by the trade winds (especially when the sea is calm, in April and May or October and November), this vast archipelago offers fantastic opportunities for island-hopping on a sailboat or underwater cruises. And the offer of an intensely romantic destination goes well beyond relaxation on the islands' beaches, splendid spas and dinners by candlelight in dream-like settings. There is Fregate Island Private, for example, a former pirate outpost (some people still believe it holds buried treasures) that has become the chicest private island resort in the Indian Ocean; not only does it have 16 villas and the incredible Banyan Hill Estate, each with its private pool, but it also boasts seven beaches, a population of 2000 giant tortoises and 100 species of birds, an organic tropical garden, and a museum of the islands' history. What's more, it is in the forefront of ambitious conservation projects.

180 / 181 - At sunset the granite formations of the famous Anse Source d'Argent beach turn pink and orange, while the breeze ripples the leaves of the palm trees that are curved due to the trade winds. This beach lies on the island of La Digue, the fourth largest in the Seychelles archipelago, named after the ship of French explorer Marc-Joseph du Fresne, who came here in 1768.

181 - Everything is ready for a barbecue (for two) on one of the beaches of Fregate Island Private. The philosophy of this resort dictates that its guests' most romantic desires are satisfied.

The Masai Mara

Kenya

182 - Surrounded by her cubs, a lioness rests after hunting for food. This is a common sight for those on a safari in Masai Mara National Reserve in Kenya, which consists of an area of 583 square miles between the Serengeti Plain in Tanzania and Rift Valley. The park boasts one of the highest populations of large cats in Africa, and, naturally, of their prey, which include zebras, gnu, and various species of gazelles.

183 - A safari in a hot-air balloon (which always concludes with an outdoor champagne breakfast) is one of the best adventures one may have in Africa.

"Observing a Masai warrior is a fine sight," wrote author Karen Blixen in *Out of Africa*. 'These young men have, to the utmost extent, that particular form of intelligence which we call chic; daring, and wildly fantastical as they seem, they are still unswervingly true to their own nature, and to an immanent ideal. Their style is not an assumed manner, nor an imitation of a foreign perfection; it has grown from the inside and is an expression of the race and its history..." You will certainly agree with the great Danish author when you meet a Masai wrapped in a fiery red mantle and decorated with beads walking proudly and alone in the Masai Mara savannah, his ancestral home. You will wonder where he is going, so disdainful of any danger (after all, large beasts of prey live here), since you see no possible destination anywhere on the horizon of this vast plain. This young, tall slender warrior will seem to be the true king of Africa, even more so than the lion.

Meeting the Masai – especially if you go visit one of the villages inhabited by this semi-nomadic pastoral population – will certainly be one of the climactic moments of a safari in the Masai Mara National Reserve, the largest in Kenya and the one with the greatest number of animals. The park is bound on one side by the Oloololo Escarpment and on the other by Serengeti National Park in Tanzania. It is is included in the great seasonal migration of the gnu, and has a large population of large felines, hippopotami, and rhinoceroses. But above all it is the territory, which, more than any other on this continent, best represents white man's fascination with the wilderness of Africa in an age when safaris were first and foremost a great romantic adventure, and a privilege for the very few. One of the first 'victims' of *mal d'Afrique* was the American Charles Cottar, who also understood that this 'illness' could be profitable. He arrived in Kenya in 1909, spellbound by the travel accounts of President Theodore Roosevelt; 10 years later he founded the first safari service company by pitching a camp with tents in the southeastern area of the Masai Mara. Now the property of his great grandchildren, Cottar's 1920s Camp is *the* place to stay in order to relive the experiences of Karen Blixen or Hemingway (both of whom stayed here). Here you can enjoy the atmosphere of (nearly) a century ago, tents, veritable 'canvas palaces,' with extremely elegant and romantic furnishings, Persian rugs, and fine dinners served by efficient, friendly waiters in a communal tent illuminated by dozens of silver candelabras. After a long day on the savannah, you can relax here and listen to the gripping tales of 'bygone days.' Like the story of the visit of the Duchess of York, who arrived with four trunks full of clothes, or of the mythical Charles Cottar himself, who survived attacks by an elephant, a buffalo and – three times – a leopard, before being killed at the age of 66 by a rhinoceros when he was only a few steps away from his camp.

184 *top* - "Observing a Masai warrior is a fine sight," Karen Blixen once wrote. These proud men who walk so elegantly have learned to live with the fauna of the Masai Mara, their ancestral land.

184 *bottom* - It is impossible not to suffer from *mal d'Afrique* after viewing a blazing sunset over the savannah, an intense and thrilling experience.

185 *top* - The elegant communal area of Cottar's 1920s Camp, situated in a private reserve of about 2500 hectares next to the Maasai Mara.

185 *bottom* - Calling them tents is almost an insult for they are more like sumptuous canvas palaces... In fact, in the nearly 100 years of its existence, Cottar's 1920s Camp has played host to the cream of European nobility, American presidents, and famous authors.

Serengeti
Tanzania

Now known the world over as a term for the most thrilling and rewarding adventure in the Black Continent, *safari* is a word in Swahili, the lingua franca of East Africa. Translated, it is 'journey.' Thus a safari, or better, *the* safari is literally the grand annual migration of 2 million gnu and about 300,000 zebras and antelopes in search of the greenest pastures in the immense ecosystem that encompasses the Serengeti and the Masai Mara plains, which lie in Tanzania and Kenya respectively. Having the privilege of watching what is the greatest mass movement in the animal world – your safari that follows *the* safari – is akin to visiting the set of a *National Geographic* documentary film. In recent years, in fact, the trek has been monitored in real time on the Web, granting viewers the certainty of being in the right place at the right time. From December to May the gnu gather in the marvelous crater of Ngorongoro, where they mate; then, when the grass covering the caldera begins to dry, they head north, towards the huge Serengeti and Masai Mara plain, which, abounding in waterways, helps them survive the dry season.

In November the moment arrives to make the same trek in the opposite direction, following a cycle that has been repeated for thousands, or perhaps even millions, of years.

You can follow this immense winding procession of animals in a jeep in order to have a 'wide-angle' view, or you can take in the entire plain by embarking on a safari in a small airplane, or even better, floating beneath a hot-air balloon. But, believe it or not, to experience the most unforgettable scenes of the entire migration, you must be in the front row, so to speak, on the banks of the Grumeti River at the end of June. For the gnu, zebra, and antelope, crossing this river – an act that can last hours or even days – is the most dangerous stretch of the journey, for two reasons: not only are the currents strong, but waiting in ambush are predators – from large felines and crocodiles to vultures and marabou that feed on carrion. Knowing instinctively that the migrating animals are most vulnerable during the crossing they simply wait for them, sure of enjoying a hearty meal. Observing this massacre along the Grumeti

186 / 187 - The greatest African show (in which the lion too plays a role) is the term for the largest mass migration in the animal world, when 2 million gnu and 300,000 zebras and antelopes move to greener pastures every year. For these creatures the most dangerous phase is the crossing of the Grumeti River in the Serengeti Plain.

River makes you understand the merciless laws of nature and the concept of the survival of the fittest; it is a spectacle that provokes strong reactions, to say the least.

Such an experience deserves an equally intense conclusion: the one offered by the luxury Singita Serengeti Camps. The name, *singita*, or 'place of miracles,' is quite apt as it succeeds in transforming a safari that reveals life and death on the wildest savannah into an incredibly romantic vacation.

188 - Guests rise early in the morning when large animals are most active in order to participate in a thrilling 'game drive' on the Grumeti Reserve, located in the northern section of the Serengeti Plain. On their return, they are given a warm welcome with a table laid with a sumptuous breakfast outdoors in the shade of acacia trees.

189 - In the wild savannah of the Serengeti-Maasai Mara ecosystem, the Singita Serengeti Camps are truly oasis of luxury. The tents are richly furnished, evoking the time when safaris were fashionable among the European elite.

Nosy Be
Madagascar

190 - A Robinson Crusoe-like but very chic vacation awaits you in the fantastic Mitsio archipelago, which crowns Nosy Be, the famous 'scented island' off the northwest coast of Madagascar. While Nosy Be, with its coconut and ylang-ylang plantations, has a colonial atmosphere, its smaller 'sisters' lie in the domain of nature, populated by fishermen communities.

191 - An aerial view of Tsarabanjina; bordered by stretches of coral reefs, this island is a temple of biodiversity, both terrestrial and subaquatic.

Cinnamon and cocoa, vanilla and coffee, frangipane and pepper. And above all, ylang-ylang, an aphrodisiac essence extracted from tiny yellow flowers that have contributed to the huge success of Chanel No. 5. This fusion of scents saturates the air and gives rise to an intensely pleasurable feeling of dizziness in all those who go to Nosy Be, the 'scented island' lying in the Mozambique Channel close to the northwestern tip of Madagascar. Although its name in the Malagasy language means 'big island,' it is really a small paradise blessed with a climate that oscillates between 68 and 86 degrees Fahrenheit for the entire year and a constant breeze that mitigates the humicity typical of the Tropics.

Nosy Be's topography is so varied that it is a sort of miniature Madagascar, with sugar cane and coffee plantations and gardens full of fragrant flowers and spices flanked by tall basalt mountains, forests, and magnificent beaches bordered by palm and baobab trees. The sea here is a veritable inventory of every shade of blue, from aquamarine to cobalt. For better or worse, Nosy Be is also the wealthiest and most European province in Madagascar, as can be seen in the buildings of its colorful principal city, Andoany (which everyone here insists on calling by its French name, Hell-Ville), as well as in the many (perhaps too

many) beaches overrun with tourists. Be that as it may, the magical atmosphere and scents of Nosy Be are inseparable from the neighboring constellation of islets that frame it, from Nosy Komba, the nearest one, where you can go in a dugout canoe through a thick forest populated by lively lemurs, up to the archipelago of the Mitsio Islands, which are simply splendid both above and under water thanks to a barrier reef teeming with multicolored fish.

Among these last-named islands, Tsarabanjina – considered sacred because it is the site of the tomb of the legendary king of the Mitsio Islands, Sakalava, to which local fishermen bring honey, fruit and rum as offerings – is home to the resort of the same name, which, with its 25 stunning and exclusive thatched villas facing the sea, has raised the standard of all-inclusive vacation packages by quite a degree. Besides five-star hospitality – including an impressive wine and champagne list – it offers facilities for snorkeling and diving, a tour with a naturalist to discover the marine and terrestrial animals on this island (the world's smallest species of chameleon has been discovered here), and catamarans for exploring the nearby, splendid atoll of Les Quatres Frères. And, naturally, a magical atmosphere scented with flowers and contagious sensuality.

192 - Amid tropical vegetation, the splendid villas of the Tsarabajina island resort are the 'last luxury stop' before entering a wild environment. Their architecture and materials respect local stylistic traditions. This marvelous island is deemed sacred because it holds the tomb of the legendary King Sakalava.

193 - Contemporary chic furnishings in the Tsarabanjina resort, which also has a wonderful spa and massage studio on the beach. The island enjoys mild weather all year round and is a perfect vacation destination for honeymooners.

 # Mauritius
Republic of Mauritius

194 - Mauritius is another ideal place for a honeymoon. Although surrounded by remarkable beaches, no other along the island's entire perimeter is comparable to the bay at Le Touessrok with Île aux Cerfs and Îlot Mangénie, a private island retreat exclusive to guests.

195 - Sunset on Le Morne Brabant, the 1824-foot basalt massif covered with vegetation that dominates a turquoise lagoon on the southwestern tip of the island. One of the rarest plants in the world, the *Hibiscus fragilis* or mandrinette grows only here.

"You gather the idea that Mauritius was created first, and then heaven; and that heaven was copied after Mauritius," wrote Mark Twain – an author who cannot be accused of being sentimental – in his travel journal. This marvelous island suspended in the Indian Ocean between Africa and Asia is the setting of *Paul and Virginia*, Bernardin de Saint-Pierre 19th-century romance that in French-speaking countries rivals Shakespeare's *Romeo and Juliet*. Given these premises, it is not surprising that today many couples from all over the world choose romantic Mauritius as the venue for the momentous "I do."

The island abounds in wedding-planning agencies that organize the ceremony (including the bureaucratic paperwork) at various sites: on white beaches, beneath the shade of palm trees, before a wonderful sunset, on the prow of a sailboat, in front of a long pond blooming with giant water lilies in the historic Pamplemousses Botanical Garden, on the patio of a colonial house, and even under water. As if this were not enough, the island has fairy-tale place names that come to the aid of spouses-to-be: Belle Mare, Sans Souci, Plaisance, and Bois Chéri.

Mauritius offers a wide range of high-class resorts located along the coastline for your honeymoon or unforgettable vacation. And while all of these have lovely beaches protected by the coral reef, excellent service, spas for demanding hedonists, and ethnic-chic architecture, none can rival the magical location of the elegant Le Touessrok, which offers its clients exclusive use of the magnificent private islet of Îlot Mangénie for enjoying Robinson Crusoe-like experiences.

Although its beaches seem to be the main attraction, the magic of Mauritius can also be found far from the seaside: the lively capital, Port Louis, which boasts colonial architecture and Hindu temples (most of the hospitable population hails from the Indian subcontinent); patches of preserved tropical forest; Black River Gorges National Park and the stunning geological formations at Chamarel, where volcanic rock is imbued with color ranging from ocher to indigo. And finally, the beautiful green expanse of the sugar cane plantations that cover half the island's surface.

Along with high-class tourism, the major component of the Mauritian economy is sugar production. Indeed, 50% of the island's energy needs is currently provided by plants that transform sugar cane waste into ethyl alcohol. Thus even the electricity and gasoline here are sweet.

Victoria Falls

Zambia/Zimbabwe

Here is some advice that you may appreciate for the rest of your life: make sure to come here between February and May, during full moon. One evening, without telling your partner anything, invite him or her to take a walk to one of the balconies with a panoramic view of the world's largest waterfall (roughly a mile wide and 354 feet high). On those magical nights when the moon is a perfect circle, its bright rays create here – and only here the most incredible sight: a moonlit rainbow. This is only to be expected. After all, Victoria Falls is the place that the indigenous Kololo people call Mosi-oa-Tunya, 'the smoke that thunders,' based on the dense spray of vaporized water produced by the Zambezi River as it plunges from the Makgadikgadi Pan into the basalt gorges below with a deafening noise. And that 'smoke,' which is visible at a distance of 31 miles, is the white sheet on which is printed the most ephemeral and romantic natural phenomenon. In 1855, the Scottish explorer David Livingstone was the first European to discover the falls, but did not manage to see the rainbow. Nevertheless, as he wrote in his diary, he was so struck by the sight of the falls that he claimed that it "the most marvelous place I have ever seen in Africa."

Protected by two adjacent national parks, *Mosi-oa-Tunya* and Victoria Falls, which occupy an area of more than 19,700 acres extending from Zambia to Zimbabwe, the falls and the territory surrounding them are a hymn to both the overwhelming power of nature and the story of the great explorers of the Black Continent. And this is precisely how you should experience the place, dividing your time between wild and exciting adventures and moments of dreamlike contemplation. Essential in the first category is to go rafting among the rapids of the Zambesi River, bungee jumping on the falls, or trekking on an elephant's back while checking out zebras, giraffes, gnu, impalas, monkeys and (naturally) crocodiles. As for meditation, the most fascinating way to practice it is on a slow boat ride to the marvelous islands that dot the river, or by sipping champagne at sunset on a steam train that was commissioned in the early 20th century by

196 / 197 - View of the Zambezi River, which widens (forming islands, then branches out into canals) after plunging from Makgadikgadi Pan into the basalt ravines below as astounding Victoria Falls. The water makes a deafening noise and produces 'smoke' or vaporized spray visible from 31 miles away, which is why the indigenous population calls the falls Mosi-oa-Tunya, 'the smoke that thunders.'

198 - Named after the person who 'discovered' Victoria Falls, the Royal Livingstone Hotel provides its guests with an atmosphere evoking the history of the exploration of the heart of Africa and Victorian colonial pomp.

the British magnate Cecil Rhodes, and which marks the beginning of the age of tourism in the heart of Africa. Finally, the place to spend the night during a full moon or not is the Royal Livingstone Hotel, in the heart of the town in Zambia named after the great explorer who 'discovered' the falls, a hotel where the atmosphere is a perfect combination of African mysteries and Victorian colonial pomp.

199 - In addition to granting visitors the pleasure of rafting the rapids of the Zambezi River or bungee jumping over the falls, the national parks of Mosi-oa-Tunya and Victoria Falls offer them extraordinary opportunities for taking safaris on foot.

The Moremi Game Reserve
Botswana

In the space of a typical day, the fingers of two hands (and often only of one) are enough to count the number of humans you may come across in this region. By the same token, it is impossible to make an inventory of the lechwe; the resident population of these large antelopes with red coats is roughly 60,000.

Furthermore, there are in total about 30,000 buffaloes and elephants; thanks to their habit of living in large and sociable groups, you can most probably spot at least 20 at any one glance. And here it is practically too easy to take photographs of lionesses hunting prey, or, together with their cubs and lazy male lion pack leader, sinking their teeth into the day's meal.

As for hippopotami and crocodiles, the problem – if any – is not to get too close to them while navigating in a *mokoro*, the traditional canoe of the indigenous Batswana people.

In short, during a safari in the Moremi Game Reserve there are far too many exciting experiences to be counted, even if you leave aside the thrill of traveling beneath a brilliant starry sky, when you may very well spot a leopard, the proudest and most solitary of nocturnal predators.

At night, the area of Moremi is so vast and powerful that it may obliterate – for the entire vacation – your perception of the existence of the 'real, outside world.' Yet Moremi – so wild and removed from everything and everybody that it can only be reached by a tiny airplane – occupies barely one-fifth of the Okavango Delta, the large river that never actually empties into the sea because its huge mass of water ends up evaporating and transpiring in the sand of the Kalahari Desert, but only after creating the fan-like shape of one of the largest inland deltas in the world, a fluid and changeable landscape of intersecting canals, infinite islands, and stretches of papyrus and curious *Kigelia africana* or sausage trees.

Even during the dry season from June to October, when the Delta is at its maximum splendor (as is the flow of tourists), the sensation of being in a primeval world remains strong, a feeling mitigated only by the luxury – equally and marvelously timeless – of the handful of safari camps scattered in the Moremi area, each one hidden from the others. The most exclusive is the picturesque Little Mombo, which welcomes and pampers only 6 guests at a time in a perfect, romantic fluvial oasis.

200 - The *mokoro*, the traditional canoe of the indigenous Batsawana population, was originally carved from the trunk of a kigel a tree. Today, however, it is made of fiberglass, but is still the smoothest means for gliding through and exploring the labyrinth of canals in the Okavango Delta.

201 - The exclusive Little Mombo Camp lies in an idyllic fluvial oasis, an area of the Moremi Reserve rich in fauna, so much so that it is not difficult to spot even the elusive leopard.

202 *top* - The greatest thrill of a safari on an elephant's back at sunset – like at Abu Camp – is to see large groups of elephants drinking. The number of these pachyderms and buffaloes in the Okavango Delta amounts to about 30,000.

202 *bottom* - At Little Mombo Camp – an exclusive camp that accommodates only 6 people at a time – each couple enjoys a private veranda with a panoramic view.

203 *top* - It seems almost inconceivable that in a place as remote as the Moremi Reserve – at the heart of the delta and accessible only by a small Cessna airplane – one can enjoy an experience that is this wild yet also this luxurious. What makes it possible here are the elegant suites, the gourmet cuisine, and the expertise of its safari guides.

203 *bottom* - The lounge of the Little Mombo Camp is an ideal place from which to observe local fauna while enjoying a cocktail. This lodge lies on Chief's Island, so named because it is dedicated to the leader of the Batswana tribe.

Kruger National Park
South Africa

204 *top* - One of the most tender images one might photograph during a game drive: a lioness leading her cubs to a pool to drink.

204 *bottom* - A knotty tree trunk dominates the comfortable king-sized bed in one of the suites of the Sabi Sabi Reserve Lodge, as if to remind guests that nature always rules here. Next to Kruger National Park, this private reserve gives visitors the opportunity to observe the Big Five.

205 - The rangers at the Sabi Sabi Game Reserve are entirely familiar with the territory and habits of its animals; thanks to them, visitors may observe the leopards, which are usually active at night.

Whoever has taken part in an African safari knows what the Big Five are. But have you ever stopped to ask why the lion, leopard, elephant, rhinoceros, and buffalo are called thus? Why have the hippopotamus and giraffe been excluded? After all, they are really large animals as well. Well, the term was granted to these creatures because they are the five most dangerous to hunt. And you do need to be very careful and attentive when approaching these animals during a 'hunt' – which, fortunately, only involves shooting photographs.

Furthermore, people tend to get awe-struck when, traveling along their tracks in an off-road vehicle in Kruger National Park, they find themselves facing the largest of these creatures, the elephants. This is partly because the ones that live here are among the most majestic on the continent with curved tusks nearly 10 feet long. These pachyderms abound in the park and have been allowed to reproduce undisturbed.

Moreover, Kruger park, with its 4,942,107 acres, is not only the largest protected area in South Africa, but also the oldest. The year 1898, at a time when few people were concerned about the ethical problems of hunting big African game, marked the establishment of the Sabi Game Reserve, the nucleus of which was expanded over time by a government campaign to enhance environmental awareness and which eventually led to the founding of the national park in 1926.

With a population of 147 species of mammals, 114 of reptiles, 34 of amphibians, 49 of fish, 507 of bird, as well as 336 of tall trees and bushes, along with, curiously enough, numerous paleo-anthropological finds, including fascinating rock carvings, the park is simply remarkable.

Next to this government-run area are others rich in fauna: Klaserie, Timbavati, Thornybush, Mala Mala, Sabi Sand and Sabi Sabi. Taken together these are the largest private wild game reserves in the world. The first established was Sabi Sabi, which for the past 30 years has offered what all its visitors call 'the safari of a lifetime.' Here you can take part in game drives early in the morning and evenings.

Early afternoon, on the other hand, is the time to take an equally exciting safari on foot as you hunt for the Little Five: the ant lion, leopard tortoise, elephant shrew, buffalo weaver, and rhino beetle. In the intervals between one adventure and the next, you can experience the 'wild' luxury of a charming lodge where you will be treated like royalty: aperitifs next to the swimming pool (with a view of a pond where giraffes and antelopes go to drink), a gourmet dinner around a fire, and enjoyable and relaxing spa treatments.

The Namib Desert

Namibia

206 - Called number 45 because it lies 45 kilometers along the road that connects the Sesriem entrance to Namib-Naukluft National Park with Sossusvlei, this is the most photographed sand dune in the world. 557 feet high, it is best seen at dawn and sunset, when the sand is permeated with fiery colors. Though seemingly uninhabitable, the desert has a large population of oryxes, the largest African antelopes.

207 - The nearly metaphysical spectacle of the famous Dead Vlei plain, dotted with black acacia trees that have been dead for at least eight centuries.

The world's tallest sand dune, Big Daddy, is 127 feet high. Climbing to the top is quite a feat, or nearly so. Walking as your feet sink into the sand is no joke, especially when considering that the temperature here drops very low before dawn but then reaches 104° Fahrenheit in no time at all. However, if you want to take a photograph of Big Daddy home with you, it's best to climb up its 'better half,' Big Mama, which is a bit shorter, and which affords a spectacular panoramic view of the Dead Vlei (dead marsh), a plain of parched soil dotted with pitch-black trunks of acacia trees, dead for at least 800 years.

If you turn towards the opposite direction you will see Naravlei, another pan whose name derives from the abundance of *nara*, plants bearing a melon-like fruit, which, in this extremely arid climate, serves as the main source of food for the animals living here – including the majestic oryxes (the largest African antelopes) with their incredibly long horns, the springboks, jackals, and ostriches.

However, the record for most photographed dune is held by the one identified simply as Number 45: shaped like a perfect pyramid, its pink sand takes on a dazzling orange-rust color at dawn and sunset.

The dunes of Sossusvlei are probably the most extraordinary tourist attraction in all of Namibia.

Once here, visitors realize how rich in emotion and allure the empty space of a desert can be. And the empty space here is truly without bounds. Sossusvlei is only a tiny part of Namib, the most ancient desert in the world, which, in turn, is part of Namib-Naukluft National Park, the largest reserve in Africa, and, the size of Switzerland, the fourth largest in the entire world. Not a bad record for a country like Namibia, which is one of the largest and least populated on the continent. As alienating as it may be – the landscape served as the oneiric, virtual reality setting of the psycho-thriller movie *The Cell* – for couples vacationing here the desert becomes a symbol of everlasting love. Indeed, there are plenty of romantic options for enjoying its marvels, which are so far from everyone and everything, be it a ride in a hot-air balloon, a champagne breakfast on the dunes, horseback riding along its picturesque canyons, or a stay in one of its beautiful lodges.

Of these, the most solitary and enticing is

Dunes Lodge, the largest in the country, which lies in the private reserve of Namib Rand, and is owned by the Namibian environmentalist Albi Bruckner. Its elegant cottages were built according to the most rigorous criteria of sustainability, with wood and canvas being the only materials. Here guests are encouraged to participate in various activities, such as safaris on foot or in small airplanes, and enjoy such delights as gourmet dinners and Star Beds, out-of-door double beds lit by lanterns so that you can spend an unforgettable night under a blanket of stars.

208 *top* - The interior of Dunes Lodge combines simplicity, sustainability, and impressive taste. Activities for guests are equally impressive: hot-air balloon rides, excursions on horseback, and nocturnal safaris on foot armed with a telescope for observing the stars in the eternally clear sky of the Namib Desert.

208 *bottom* - Situated south of Sossusvlei and next to Namib-Naukluft National Park, the Namib Rand Reserve covers an area of 200,000 hectares and is the largest private reserve in the country. It is also the home to Dunes Lodge, one of the most ambitious zero impact projects developed by Albi Brückner, an environmentalist and pioneer of nature conservation in Namibia.

209 - Having a swimming pool in one of the most arid places on our planet is truly a luxury. While remaining true to its philosophy of sustainability, the Dunes Lodge provides its guests with great comfort and epicurean pleasures. Its restaurant, for example, is deemed to offer the best gourmet meals in Namibia's entire safari circuit.

Whistler
Canada

210 *top* - The largest skiing area in North America consists of the Whistler and Blackcomb massifs. Its proximity to the Pacific coast ensures that the winter temperature never drops below 15° Celsius. The average annual snowfall, on the other hand, is 36 feet.

210 *bottom* - Nita Lake Lodge – on the banks of the glacial lake of the same name – is one of the most exclusive resorts in Canada.

211 - Consisting of two massifs, the Whistler and the Blackcomb, this is the largest skiing area in North America. Thanks to its proximity to the Pacific coast, the temperature hardly ever drops below15 degrees Celsius in winter. On the other hand, the average yearly snowfall is 36 feet.

When a group of trappers founded it in the late 19th century, they called it London because the fog that rose up from the numerous small glacial pools scattered throughout the area reminded them – in a curiously nostalgic way – of fog in the capital of their mother country.

In 1966, when this village was transformed into a ski resort, however, the original name must have seemed a bit depressing and negative, so the authorities renamed it Whistler after the typical call made by the hoary marmots that live in these mountains. And the whistle proved to be a good luck charm.

In 2010, some of the events of the Winter Olympic Games in Vancouver were held here since the splendid capital of British Columbia and Whistler are linked by one of the most panoramic highways in the world, which a little more than 70 miles long, runs from the Pacific coast to a spectacular landscape of forests and craggy peaks.

In addition, Whistler is the largest skiing region in the Americas, so vast that it claims a 'population' of 1200 ski instructors and has become a hugely popular glam locale. More celebrities appear here than snowfalls: gossip claims that the Cameron Diaz-Justin Timberlake love story took place on the ski run here, and that the rock star Seal asked top model Heidi Klum to marry him during a trip in a helicopter over the local glacier.

And though the superstar couple's love has since dissolved like snow in the hot sun, no one interested in a truly romantic vacation should be discouraged by this. Along with the thrills of skiing and other snow adventures, Whistler will also satisfy your après-ski desires, thanks to its many gourmet restaurants that range from the marvelously 'infernal' cuisine of chef Gordon Ramsay's establishment to a host of others that interpret the delights of the school of haute cuisine known as Pacific Rim, of which two of the most fabulous dishes are Vancouver Bay oysters and buffalo fillet. And while in the restaurants champagne flows like a river, luxury is the rule of the many hotels here, first and foremost Nita Lake Lodge, which, with its Zen architecture reflected in a glacial lake and its fantastic spa, is considered one of the ten most exclusive resorts in Canada.

Whistler is so special that it is worthwhile going there in summer, when the ski area becomes an immense Disneyland for walks in a natural setting and adventures on a mountain bike. Furthermore, from May to October you can go to Whistler 'ecologically,' that is, on board the Whistler Mountaineer, a train that runs along the first leg of the Canadian Rocky Mountains railway line, and thus take a journey that *National Geographic* has referred to as "one of the experiences that change your life."

In Montana
USA

212 *top* - From Lookout Rock one can spot the Paws Up ranch, a 15,000-hectare area in Greenough, in the legendary Blackfoot River Valley, once explored by Lewis and Clark. Here you can enjoy a true cowboy lifestyle, riding with the herds of cattle, fishing and making excursions to nearby Glacier National Park.

212 *bottom and* 213 - The elegant hospitality of the tents for guests at The Resort at Paws Up is as unexpected as it is welcome in such a 'wild' state as Montana. These canvas suites are located near the banks of the Blackfoot River in a bucolic and idyllic setting.

"I'm in love with Montana," John Steinbeck once wrote. "For other states I have admiration, respect, recognition, even some affection. But with Montana it is love. And it's difficult to analyze love when you're in it." Actually, this is a difficult question not only for one of the leading 20th-century American authors. While all the other states in the Union have an official name, Montana has reached no real consensus on the matter. In fact, it has several nicknames: Big Sky Country, The Treasure State, Land of Shining Mountains, and The Last Best Place. And all of these appeallations are perfect. 'Big sky' is what covers the infinite space of an immense territory with a surface area of over 147,000 square miles and a population of little more than 1 million (much less, in fact, than that of the wild fauna; no other state, for example, has such a large number of grizzly bears),and which imparts a sense of eternity that is difficult to experience elsewhere. As for the 'treasures' and 'shining mountains,' these are the 24 ranges that form part of the Rocky Mountains, some of which lie in Yellowstone National Park and Glacier National Park. And finally, Montana is the Last Best Place because its scenery has remained unchanged since the time of the expedition led by Lewis and Clark. In 1803 President Thomas Jefferson sent these two officers on an exploratory mission to discover a practicable route into and through the Northwest to the Pacific Ocean – a feat that laid the foundations for the birth of the modern United States.

Montana is still the last frontier; it was the venue of the Battle of Little Big Horn, arguably the most famous in the history of the Indian wars, in which General Custer's troops suffered a devastating defeat. Eleven Native American tribes still reside in the state, and a visit to a Cheyenne or Niitsitapi (better known as Blackfeet) reservation, especially during the pow-wow ceremonies, is an impressive experience. Last but not least, the plains of Montana are in most people's minds the Western setting par excellence, a place where they can have a cowboy vacation on a ranch, perhaps on a horse accompanying the seasonal cattle-drive to greener pastures.

Now you might object that a vacation here is more likely to live up to the dream of the male half of a couple, which has fed on John Wayne movies during its youth. Yet, surprisingly enough, a house in the prairie can be extremely romantic, particularly if you reserve a place in a ranch such as The Resort at Paws Up. Covering an area of 37,000 acres in Blackfoot River valley, a short distance from spectacular Glacier National Park, this resort offers luxury accommodations amid wild nature and is an ideal place for couples, with activities such as horseback riding and excursions, adventurous rafting and thrilling abseiling, that is, double-rope descents from the rock face where Lewis and Clark found refuge during a terrible storm. In April this ranch becomes the venue of a roundup of American cowgirls during an incredible week when the Far West is dominated by the 'gentle sex.'

Nantucket and Martha's Vineyard

USA

214 - Two beaches, one overlooking the Atlantic and the other facing more placid Nantucket Bay, crown the extremely elegant Wauwinet, a hotel with a nautical atmosphere on an island famous for its whale hunters. But then again, on Nantucket even fishermen huts on the piers are chic; many, in fact, have become seemingly modest 'hideaways' for Boston and New York high society.

215 - Together with sailing, fishing (including lobster and clam fishing) is one of the favorite sports among the habitués of Nantucket.

They tried, but their request to secede
from the state of Massachusetts – which they
discussed in Washington in 1977 – was dismissed
with unequivocal refusal. And at bottom the
decision made by the country's highest authority
was received in a spirit of pragmatism: the
residents of Nantucket and Martha's Vineyard
knew quite well that their islands would continue
to be part of a distinct world. Indeed, they are
the epitomy of the contemporary version of the
American Dream. Washed by the Gulf Stream,
which ensures warm summers that last until
October, the islands lie a short distance from the
East Coast, on a level with the peninsular 'hook'
of Cape Cod. But arrival there (roughly an hour
by boat, or better yet, by private jet) means you
have… 'arrived.'

Surprisingly, the secret of the success of
these two romantic vacation sites for the rich
& famous – from the entire Kennedy clan, the
'guardians' of what is commonly known as The
Vineyard, to such celebrities as Madonna and
Robert De Niro along with Pulitzer Prize-winning
authors – lies in their very chic reserve and
absolute respect for privacy.

Martha's Vineyard is larger and woodier.
Nantucket is wilder and more 'Atlantic,' and is,
in fact, home to a colony of seals at the tip of a
promontory and serves as one of the world's chief
whaling centers.

Both islands have extremely captivating
seascapes, shores dotted with lighthouses that
seem to emerge from an Edward Hopper painting,
as well as enchanting beaches. The Vineyard also
has a series of sandstone cliffs whose colors
change throughout the day. At the top of one
of the cliffs is Gay Head reservation, where the
Wampanoag Indians, natives of these coasts
and those of all Massachusetts, have maintained
their traditions, such as making splendid pink
wampum charms.

Half the land on these islands is protected
by law and houses must conform to the size
and style set by severe regulations. Indeed,
despite the fact that both islands serve as
summer 'annexes' to Manhattan, Washington
D.C., and Hollywood, celebrities must be content,
so to speak, to stay in homes and hotels that
outwardly, at least, appear quite modest. And
while a top attraction on Martha's Vineyard is the

216 - This summer sunset on the Edgartown promontory, dominated by one of the five lighthouses along the perimeter of Martha's Vineyard, has all the poetry of a painting by Edward Hopper.

216 / 217 - The beaches at Martha's Vineyard are bordered by sandstone cliffs. Being part of the tribal land of the Wampanoag Indians, they have become a reserve.

charming, brightly colored, Hänsel and Gretel-like houses built 100 years ago in the Methodist enclave within the village of Oak's Bluff, Nantucket is nicknamed Gray Lady due to the elegant color of its wooden houses after merely one winter's exposure to salinity. Gray is also the color of the Wauwinet of Nantucket, an exclusive hotel that epitomizes 'minimal luxury' and serves as a refuge for sea dogs, offering them many fine amenities, including rides on boats or in vintage automobiles.

San Francisco
USA

218 - The lights of the San Francisco skyline glitter like spangles; the city's famous profile has even appeared on the phenomenally huge hat worn in the legendary musical *Beach Blanket Babylon*, which has been performed in the city every evening for the past 40 years. Among the treasures of this most liberal city in the States are the Painted Ladies, old pastel colored Victorian houses that line Alamo Square.

219 - The Golden Gate Bridge – emerging as if by magic from the layer of low clouds that envelops the bay – is the most iconic 'postcard' image of San Francisco.

The most bizarre skyline in San Francisco is the one reproduced faithfully on a hat – with a diameter of at least 13 feet and a height of over 6 feet – worn by one of the stars in the grand finale of *Beach Blanket Babylon*, a spectacle designated as the longest-playing musical in history by the *Guinness Book of World Records*. The show opened on 7 June 1974, with 8 performances per week, at the charming Fugazi Theatre in the Italian quarter of North Beach. The rococo-style interior has a seating capacity of 393 and its audience is usually divided equally among tourists and locals. Some of the latter have seen this scintillating performance 50 times, certain that they will always experience new sensations.

It couldn't be otherwise. An evening among the spangles and amazing hats worn by the actors of *BBB*, as its *aficionados* call it, is one of the 'musts' of a vacation in San Francisco because the show is able to make viewers dream and laugh until tears come to their eyes. And come to think of it, this is the very nature of the city itself, the craziest and most liberal in the United States, where every generation has given rise to its own legends: the beatniks of the 1950s, the flower children of the 1970s, the cybernauts of the 1990s. *En passant*, mention should be made of the fact that here, a long, long time ago, a certain Levi Strauss 'invented' jeans, consequently revolutionizing young people's attire throughout the world. One might continue by mentioning

that the city's energy is as evident in places such as the Castro district and in the demonstrations that have marked the history of the gay rights movement, as it is in the huge parks and buildings – such as the astounding California Academy of Sciences designed by Renzo Piano – that relate the story of the green revolution in a city with one of most determined, ecologically aware populations in the world. Moreover, this movement has triggered the establishment of many organic markets and gourmet restaurants, which in a country full of fast food, are the standard bearers of slow-food philosophy.

San Francisco is a city steeped in references. You should explore and discover it by losing yourself in its neighborhoods, either on foot or on the vertiginous uphill climbs of its iconic cable cars, one of the city's many symbols. Here you can experience the allure of the Orient in a marvelous Chinatown and relive the Gilded Age by taking in the town's splendid Victorian and Edwardian architecture, first and foremost its so-called Painted Ladies – the wooden houses with pastel colors lining Alamo Square. Next, you can feel as though you are in a famous movie, from mysteries based on Dashiell Hammett's novels to *Escape from Alcatraz* (the notorious former island prison in the bay opposite one of the city's most popular tourist attractions, Fisherman's Wharf), not to mention the masterpieces of Alfred Hitchcock, who chose the city as the location for several of his films.

220 - A panoramic view of Cavallo Point, one of the most romantic lodges on the West Coast, which lies near famous Golden Gate Bridge, in a National Recreation Area of ecological and historic importance.

Scenes in *The Birds* were shot in San Francisco, and the climax of *Vertigo* was filmed beneath the famous orange-colored Golden Gate Bridge, the highlight of beautiful San Francisco Bay. Much of the territory on either side of the bridge consists of parks and protected areas that include historic monuments and interesting natural sites. On the outer side of the bridge, near an old fort in the neighboring coastal town of Sausalito, is Cavallo Point, an elegant lodge for those in love with intimate love nests offering wonderful views, and in which you can relax after your urban adventures. And don't forget the romantic and epicurean sights of Northern California, such as the vineyards of world-famous Napa Valley.

221 - A short drive north will take you to the softly rolling hills of Napa Valley, world-famous for its many prestigious wineries (open for wine-tasting) and gourmet restaurants.

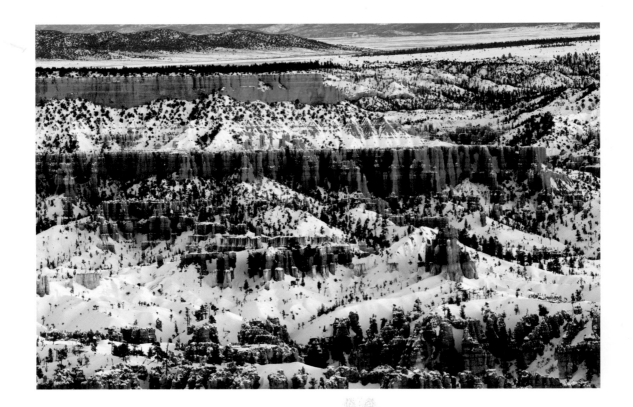

Moab
USA

222 *top and* 223 - Is it more exciting to visit the major parks of the American Southwest in summer or winter? No agreement exists on this point. What is certain is that after a snowfall, the *hoodoos* (the pinnacles shaped by erosion) of the amphitheater-shaped Bryce Canyon and the top of Grand Canyon are unforgettable. What's more, there are fewer tourists then…

222 *bottom* - A typical American Indian teepee (in an original, luxury format) and huge open space at your disposal – provided by Moab Under Canvas, a marvelous and very romantic 'camp' that serves as an ideal base for an adventurous trip to Arches and Canyonlands National Park, the land of the famous movie, *Stagecoach*.

In order for it to be classified as an 'arch,' the opening of a rock formation must be at least 3 feet long. In compliance with this criterion, 2000 have been registered in Arches National Park, while the record for the largest one – not only in the park but in the whole world – is held by the Landscape Arch, which is 306 feet long, and thus has an opening as large as a football field. Besides its arches the park also contains red sandstone formations, the results of 150 million years of floods and subsequent stages of evaporation (26 in all), telluric uplift and displacement, and immense erosion, which continues to this day. The park also has a blackish, sandy, saline bed dotted with transient pools that is, in fact, a biological crust composed of fungi, algae, lichen, and cyanobacteria (the last-mentioned being the earliest known form of life on earth).

Yet, all such 'technical' details – which must be included in any description of this park – will not prepare you for the impact made by the grandiose landscape of legendary Red Rock Country in Utah, the northern section of the Colorado Plateau, an area measuring 129,344 square miles (and extending over four states) and home to about 30 reserves and national parks, some of which are the most amazing in the United States: the Zion, Bryce Canyon, Monument Valley, and Grand Canyon, as well as Mesa Verde, which

holds the most important group of ancient pueblos or cliff dwellings of the Anasazi Indians, ancestors of the Navajos.

It is impossible to list all the destinations in this area, which can offer you the outdoor adventure of your life, but we can suggest how to experience it in a marvelously romantic fashion. First of all, go to Moab, a town incorporated in the early 20th century as a uranium mining center and later transformed into a sort of entertainment and recreational park for exciting vacations. From here you need only go a few miles to reach the entrance to Arches National Park, where you can also find a splendid resort under the stars, Moab Under Canvas. This is a luxury camp consisting of a group of tepees, the traditional cone-shaped homes of Northern Native Americans, that offers the experience of a 'western safari' for its guests. Activities include trekking both on foot and mountain bike, white-water rafting in the Green and Colorado Rivers, free-climbing excursions, and trips in hot-air balloons. Furthermore, only a short distance away is the 'land of arches' (contemplating sunset at the Delicate Arch, the rock formation that has become the symbol of Utah is an absolute must) and Canyonlands National Park, arguably even more 'extraterrestrial.' It is the largest protected area in Utah, the immensity of which can be grasped

224 - The Delicate Arch rock formation (here bathed in the magical
light of sunset) is the emblematic site of Arches National Park, which
occupies an area of 31,000 hectares near the town of Moab and boasts
about 2000 natural arches.

224 / 225 - Hunt's Mesa in Canyonlands National Park is both a surreal and
familiar landscape, since everyone has seen it in one of many Westerns.

from Grand View Point, which, at an altitude of 6080 feet, offers a total panoramic view of the mesas, sandstone terraces overlooking a network of canyons as deep as 3280 feet that create an 'alien' landscape known as the 'Island in the Sky.' This park also boasts the famous Needles, a forest of rock pinnacles that is the natural precursor of the Manhattan skyline, with colors ranging from ocher to bright red. And if this is not sufficiently 'out of this world' for your taste, you can go to the most remote area of the Canyonlands, Horseshoe Canyon, where you will find an orange rockface on which ancient native American Indians have carved and painted anthropomorphic figures, some with strange extensions resembling antennas. Some say they are extraterrestrials…

Charleston

USA

226 *top* - Enjoying the sunset on the pier of Castle Pinckney, a fort built on a promontory in 1818 to protect Charleston harbor and one that also played an important strategic role during the American Civil War.

226 *bottom* and 227 - Dawn at Boneyard Beach on Bull, the largest of the coastal islands several miles north of Charleston. While the island is part of Cape Romain National Wildlife Refuge and an open invitation for romantic walks in a natural setting, Charleston offers visitors the pleasure of an historical itinerary along the harbor that offers a view of the buildings on the Battery promenade.

The farewell scene between Rossella O'Hara and her lover, Captain Rhett Butler, is one of the most moving in the history of film-making. Taking his leave at the end of *Gone with the Wind*, Rhett – played by a divine Clark Gable – looks at Rossella intensely and says, "I'm going back to Charleston, back where I belong... I want to see if somewhere there isn't something left in life of charm and grace."

In the period captured in the film, Charleston was one of the key cities of the American Civil War. As coastal outpost of the Confederacy, it was bombarded and blockaded by Union troops, becoming the stage set of epic battles. In short, it was – and is, in the memory of Americans – one of the leading forces in the history of the United States. This peninsular city on the coast of South Carolina, between the Ashley and Cooper Rivers also boasts of other records. One of the nation's oldest libraries was founded here in 1698. It can claim the earliest theater (1736), earliest public museum (1773) and earliest golf course (1786) in the United States. In addition, the famous dance epitomizing the Roaring Twenties was named after the city. And indeed the past here is still very much alive thanks to 73 sublimely elegant and perfectly preserved houses that have become historic American monuments. Indeed, strolling through the cobblestone streets (you can also hire a gig) is akin to being in an old-time film set. Make sure to visit famous Rainbow Row, a street along the harbor lined with old pastel-colored houses, and the

Battery at the end of the peninsula. It should thus come as no surprise that Charleston is considered the most romantic city in the US, so much so that finding a hotel room on St. Valentine's Day weekend is quite a feat here.

For that matter, what could be more romantic than experiencing the atmosphere of *Gone with the Wind*? To make this even more real you must reserve a suite at Wentworth Mansion, the opulent 19th-century home of a cotton magnate converted into an elegant and quaint hotel that glistens with shiny mahogany furniture, brass fixtures, and Tiffany stained glass. This building and others in the historic section are enough to justify your visit to Charleston (which must include a dinner of typically spicy Southern cuisine by candlelight). But what really makes the city unique are its surroundings, the beaches, the coastal islands (which are now eco-tourist attractions), and large estates with cotton plantations. The last mentioned include absolute treasures such as Drayton Hall, the most perfect example of Georgian-Palladian architecture in the United States; Middleton Place, a plantation with a lavish residence and the oldest and most appealing formal gardens in the country; and Boone Hall, which, with its majestic access lined with centuries-old oak trees, is the most frequently photographed plantation in the United States, and so evocative that it is easy to imagine meeting Rossella and Rhett holding hands while strolling here.

228 *top* - A view of the majestic branches of moss-covered old oak trees (planted in 1743!) that line the access road to Boone Hall, a plantation recalling the rural heritage of the American South.

228 *bottom* - Set amid the enchanting scenery about 12 miles from Charleston, Drayton Hall is one of the best examples of Georgian-Palladian architecture in the United States.

229 - Built for a cotton magnate in the heart of Charleston, Wentworth Mansion is now an elegant hotel whose rooms feature precious mahogany furniture, brass fixtures, and Tiffany glass.

The Florida Keys
USA

230 - Little Palm Island Resort & Spa is the most private and romantic retreat in Florida, occupying the entire islet of the same name in Little Torch Key coral reef. Here you can relax on an unspoiled beach with fine white sand or practice aquatic sports in the sea with its gamut of blue hues.

231 - The marina of Islamorada, also known as the 'village of islands' because it consists of 5 islands, is the perfect place for going marlin fishing in tribute to author Ernest Hemingway, who was in love with the Keys.

105 miles long and with 42 bridges suspended over a sea that could simply not be bluer, Overseas Highway is one of those throughfares that has become part and parcel of the 'on the road' legend, and one you must travel over in a cabriolet as wind blows through your hair. The road connects Miami – a fabulous starting point thanks to the glamor and Art Deco architecture of South Beach – to Key West, the southernmost city in the continental United States. It is best to arrive just before sunset, in time to find a place in the front row of Mallory Deck for the Sunset Celebration, a show performed every single day, when the sun's descent into the Caribbean Sea is hailed with loud, and well deserved, applause.

With its many features – little caramel-colored houses, small souvenir shops, absurd T-shirts and those small visor caps that Americans on vacation seem unable to do without, dozens of cocktail bars that spew terribly loud music and invariably bear a sign that reads "Papa Hemingway drank here" (although the only actual alcoholic refuge of the legendary author of *A Farewell to Arms* is the now world-famous Sloppy Joe's) – Key West is a charmingly kitsch destination. Take all the time you need to become infected with its merry atmosphere – perhaps indulging in a 'ghost tour' to see the many famous personalities who have

lived here – without neglecting to have your fortune read with tarot cards. Curiously enough, there is a small army of fortune tellers here who have literally colonized all corners of the streets and piers, all of whom are quite adept at convincing you that all your dreams will come true. But then again, there is the possibility of a romantic vacation. The Florida Keys consist of a necklace of 1700 coralline islands, one more marvelous than the other, and all with the usual abundance of white beaches, palm trees, and fabulous sea. And while everybody can enjoy snorkeling or a bird-watching excursion at Bahia Honda Key, the most tropical island in the protected U.S. area, or a swim with dolphins and tortoises in the crystal-clear waters of Key Largo, the self-proclaimed world capital of diving, it is a privilege of the very few to bask in the idyll of Little Palm Island, a tiny paradise in the Little Torch Key coral reef, which can be reached only by boat, or better yet, by seaplane. Here lies a very exclusive resort that is one of the top ten honeymooner retreats in the country, thanks partly to a series of programmed events that are thoroughly romantic, among which are the Sandbar Sessions, magical nights beneath a full moon when major jazz musicians play on the beach, creating an unforgettable sound track for your vacation.

232 - Donated to American divers by the Cressi family in Italy (which produces diving equipment), the Christ of the Abyss lies at a depth of about 25 feet near Key Largo.

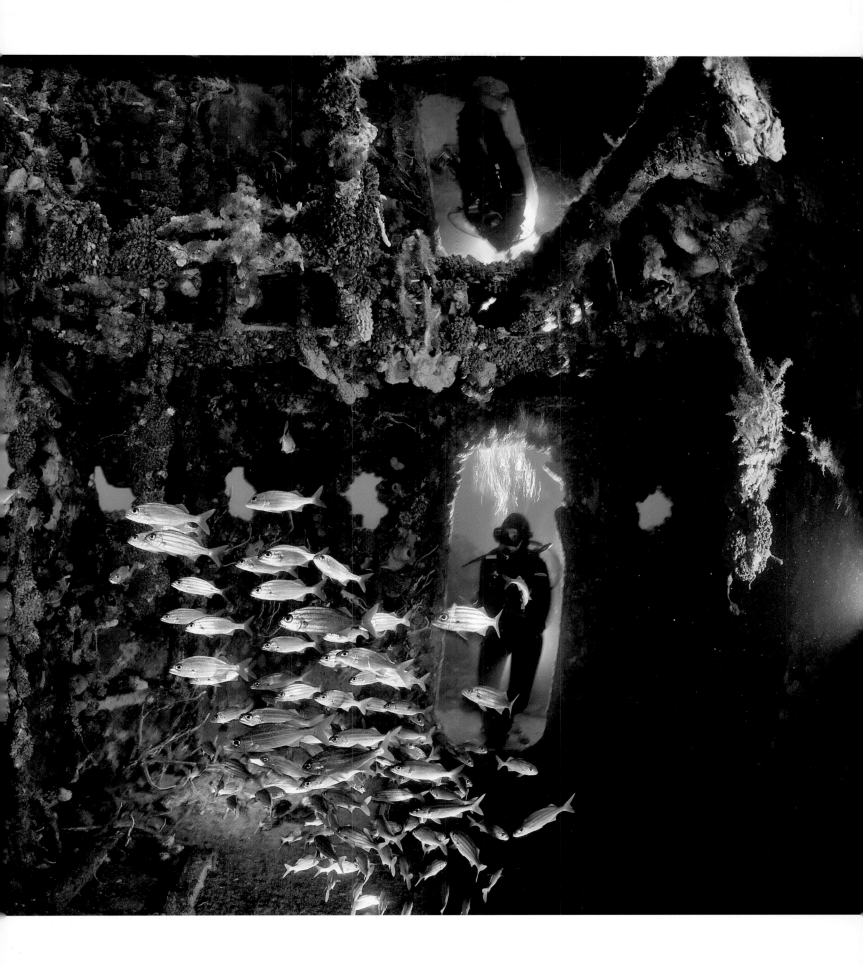

232 / 233 - The shipwreck of the *Duane*, a U.S. Coast Guard cutter that sank in the 1980s, has become a very popular home for fish. It goes without saying, that it is also one of the most thrilling diving sites in Key Largo.

Los Cabos

Mexico

234 - It is not difficult to understand why Los Cabos beach, dominated by a fascinating natural arch, has been named Playa del Amor or Lover's Beach. At the tip of Baja California there is no lack of romantic and amazingly beautiful places, both natural and man-made. Among the latter, honorable mention must go to Las Ventanas al Paraíso, the luxury resort that is a favorite among Hollywood stars (in the image the infinity pool of the resort).

235 - A whale-watching adventure: observing the movements of these huge creatures in their sanctuary, El Vizcaino Nature Reserve.

El Fin del Mundo, or Land's End: this is the name given to the rock arch jutting over the tip of the peninsula known as Baja California. This powerful monument of nature marks the exact point where the Sea of Cortez merges with the Pacific, revealing the clear-cut contrast between the turquoise waters of the former and the dark blue of the ocean. The phenomenon can be admired from a boat, at the end of an excursion that begins with the locality of Cabo San Lucas. Along this itinerary you will enjoy close-up views of whales (this sea is a cetacean sanctuary, protected by El Vizcaino Nature Reserve) and be able to observe a series of seascape scenes that are both wild and disturbing: rocks that house large colonies of pelicans and sea lions, as well as stacks and steep cliffs overlooking the sea and alternating with white beaches. Among the last mentioned, the most famous is the Playa del Amor, or Beach of Love, along the Sea of Cortez. A short sand path connects it to its twin on the opposite side of the peninsula, which is equally beautiful and inviting. Yet because it is bordered by the Pacific it has treacherous currents and in fact has earned the witty nickname 'Playa del Divorcio' (Divorce Beach).

If yours is a romantic vacation, you must by all means avoid this beach, especially since the thin strip of land of Baja California has so much more to offer, be it dream-like desert scenery dotted with cactus (to be explored with an off-road quad

bike or four-by-four vehicle) or towns that have grown into tourist centers, from the overcrowded Cabo San Lucas to the more refined San José del Cabo, ideal for an afternoon of shopping in art galleries and chic handicrafts shops. However, all this advice regarding visits either by land or sea may be of little use if you have already booked a room at Las Ventanas al Paraíso, one of the most wished-for resorts on the continent. Tucked in a remarkable natural setting between the desert and the blue sky and sea (and with constant and careful attention paid to providing sheer luxury while adhering to principles of ecological balance), this resort is truly a window on paradise. Among its habitués are many Hollywood stars – including Jessica Alba, Gwyneth Paltrow and George Clooney – who are attracted by the resort's almost obsessive protection of their privacy, a policy that has proved so effective that the gossip magazines continue to feature imaginary 'scoops' concerning famous love stories that supposedly began here.

Nonetheless, it is simply impossible not to fall in love in – and with – this fabulous resort, whose large and efficient staff includes even a Department of Romance, a team specialized in creating the most magical atmospheres for couples, from aroma-therapeutic massages in their rooms to dinners by candlelight on the cliffs, far from everything and everybody. If this is not a perfect setting for a proposal, what is?

San Miguel de Allende
Mexico

236 - A terrace with a fine panoramic view and one of the enchanting suites at L'Ôtel, the most exclusive and romantic place to stay in San Miguel de Allende, furnished in a style that has been called 'creative colonial' and decorated with exuberant paintings by local artists, all of which are for sale for those who might wish for an elegant souvenir of their dream vacation here.

237 - The magical light of sunset illuminates the picturesque historic center of San Miguel de Allende. Built on a hill at an altitude of 6233 feet, the city is dominated by a majestic cathedral, one of the most beautiful in Mexico, made in a local Neo-Gothic style that is so ornate and eccentric that it recalls Gaudí's Sagrada Família in Barcelona.

They call it *fiesta de los locos*, the fiesta of the mad, when everyone is invited to take part in the dancing procession along the virtually inaccessible streets of San Miguel de Allende wearing the most flamboyant clothes, costumes and masks imaginable. The festival takes place in June in honor of St. Anthony of Padua and the lesser known St. Pasquale Baylón, a Spanish monk and patron saint of pastry chefs and frustrated women (allegedly when people came to him to confess, the saint prescribed zabaglione as a remedy for marital difficulties). Needless to say, this procession is an explosion of colors and merriment, an event unique even in colorful Mexico. Furthermore, due to its beautiful architecture – from Baroque and Neo-Classical aristocratic residences to a hybrid Neo-Gothic cathedral, certainly as extravagant as Gaudí's Sagrada Família in Barcelona – and unusual light, San Miguel de Allende captures the Mexico that we all imagine to the nth degree.

Of the 80,000 inhabitants, about 15,000 are foreigners who now reside in this city, which lies at the exact center of Mexico, in the state of Guanajuato (no other place in the country is further from the sea). And it is thanks to a foreigner, the American artist Stirling Dickinson, that the second golden age of San Miguel de Allende began in the late 1930s. In fact, the city – founded in 1551 by a Spanish friar near a hot spring in the heart of the Parque Principal now used for washing clothes – had already enjoyed a long pperiod of splendor thanks to the veins of silver in the

vicinity of the Ruta de Plata, on which the precious metal was transported from the mines at Zacatecas to Mexico City. Later, after the country achieved independence, the city declined, so much so that when Dickinson arrived its mansions were in a state of nearly complete abandonment. The artist fell in love with the 'impoverished lady' and decided to stay there, and was appointed director of the recently established University School of Fine Arts, located in an old monastery, where David Alfaro Siqueros, a leading 20th-century Mexican artists, was a teacher. With time the city began to flourish again, attracting a heterogeneous colony of artists, some of whom even became hotel owners. This was the case with the extremely hospitable owners of L'Ôtel, an elegant, colorful and romantic refuge that is ideal for a vacation that you may hope will last forever.

Situated around a large square known as El Jardín, which is always enlivened by mariachis playing sad ballads and Indian women who sell gastronomic delights, the historic center of San Miguel de Allende is now a place where one falls in love, a city to be enjoyed by wandering among art galleries, traditional marketplaces and handicrafts workshops, or by taking advantage of the many spas offering temazcal, the Central American version of a Turkish bath, and massages with herbs from the Sierra Madre mountain range. Another option is simply to enjoy this magical, theatrical, colonial-style setting, the embodiment of what has been called the 'Old New World.'

Yucatán
Mexico

238 *top* - Chichén Itzá was the religious, cultural and economic capital of the Maya civilization in the Yucatán Peninsula. The hub of this fascinating archeological site is the Temple of Kukulcan, also known as El Castillo, one of the most famous step pyramids in Mexico. Lying opposite is another, almost equally majestic monument, the Temple of the Warriors.

238 *bottom* - Painted in Pompeii red and overlooking a splendid pool, is Hacienda Temozón, a Spanish colonial period estate converted into an elegant hotel.

239 - Arguably the most fascinating archeological site in the Yucatán Peninsula, the Maya city of Tulúm was the first to be sighted by Spanish sailors on 3 March 1517.

According to legend, the name Yucatán given by conquistadores to the sweetest peninsula in Mexico – which extends into the Caribbean Sea and is blessed with at least 270 full days of sun each year – derives from *Yuuch-ax-tann*, which in the Mayan language means 'We don't understand you.' It is said that as the Indios helplessly watched as the Spanish destroyed their temples and seized all their belongings, they repeated this above phrase with a great deal of fatalism. One could say that to this day the descendants of the ancient Maya still do not understand foreigners: why the devil do they remain packed together on a strip of sand in order to roast themselves in the sun when there is plenty of space and shade in which to spend the day?

Now known the world over as one of the most multicolored vacation capitals, the Mayan Rivera, which faces the turquoise waters of the Caribbean Sea between Cancún and Tulúm (where a majestic Mayan pyramid offering a panoramic view overlooks the sea), is a fabulous destination to which to escape cold winter. Here it is only too easy to get overwhelmed with laziness and leaving the beach only briefly for a short trip to the world-famous archeological site of Chichén Itzá. Yet, the immediate inland of the Yucatán offers truly unforgettable experiences. Here you can visit lovely estates from the time of Spanish colonization. Built on huge plots of land, these haciendas have made their owners wealthy thanks to the cultivation of

henequen, a species of agave erroneously known as sisal, derived from the name of the Yucatán port that served as the starting point for ships going to Europe with a cargo of this fiber, used to produce rope and twine. Now that sisal has been supplanted by synthetic fiber, some of the haciendas have been converted into captivating resorts. Among these, the most luxurious is the Hacienda Temozón, which welcomes its guests in a splendid Pompeii red structure with 18th-century furniture; each room has a patio with a king-size hammock and a private thermal pool. Less than an hour's drive from the sea, this hacienda is situated at a strategic point for visits to Mérida, the delightful capital of the Yucatán, as well as for side trips to the so-called Puuc Route, a road that includes the archeological sites of Uxmal, Kabah, Sayil, Klapak and Labná. From here you can also discover the marvels of Ruta de los Conventos (Route of the Monasteries), which starts at Merida and features a series of picturesque villages, each with its own Baroque religious treasure, until you arrive at the magnificent town of Izamal. Here stands the monastery of St. Anthony of Padua founded in 1561, thus the oldest in the Western Hemisphere. Twice a year, on December 8 and August 15, and against the setting of this marvelous bright yellow structure, the locals celebrate the most important festival in the Yucatán, which honors the syncretism of Christianity and ancient Mayan ritual, with the pure magic of music, colors and… margaritas.

Ambergris Caye

Belize

240 top - The depths of the extraordinary karstic sinkhole known as the Great Blue Hole were first explored in 1971 by Jacques-Yves Cousteau.

240 bottom and 241 - A diver exploring the coral reef of the Hol Chan ('little canal' in the Mayan language) Marine Reserve, an area of 3 square miles to the south of Ambergris Caye and one of the numerous spectacular diving points in the largest barrier reef of the Northern Hemisphere. A short distance from Ambergris Caye is Cayo Espanto, a private islet with an exclusive resort.

Because of their sinuous movements and elegant color, Rock Beauty, Queen Angelfish, and French Angelfish are the three species of angelfish that deserve the undisputed title of Miss Barrier Reef in Belize. Due to its stouter body (though compensated by multi-colored streaks and dots) the parrotfish takes second place in the ranking of what could be called the local subaquatic beauty contest. However, a prominent feature of this fish is a very curious habit; if you go diving or snorkeling early in the morning, you will see it asleep in a gelatinous cocoon in which it wraps itself each night in order to be protected from predators.

You may wonder what dreams it has beneath that translucent cocoon. And do fish dream? We certainly will not bet on it, but one thing is certain: for humans, at least, the largest barrier reef in the Northern Hemisphere is truly a dream, an enchanted forest of coral and gorgonians populated by a phantasmagoria of fish and a phenomenal sampling of marine life forms.

Added to this are the many essential destinations for diving and snorkeling buffs, from the famous Great Blue Hole to the spots along Lighthouse Reef and around Half Moon Caye, an islet whose very name is romantic. This is what awaits you beneath the surface of the sea.

On land, Belize is – if this were possible – even more *Unbelizeable*! This word, obviously a combination of the country's name and *unbelievable*, was coined at Ambergris Caye, Belize's largest island. And it isn't difficult to understand why.

Bordered by splendid coralline sand beaches and mangrove labyrinths, the country is literally blanketed in coconut palms. Its sole village, San Pedro, is a haven of small wooden houses, perfect for relaxation and entertainment in the most carefree and musical Caribbean style. This is where you will find the largest diving companies, as well as tourist agencies that offer 'terrestrial' adventures of all sorts.

A 'must' are forest hikes, some of which will take you to mysterious Mayan archeological sites such as Caracol and Xunantunich.

Finally, and arranged like a crown over Ambergris Caye are countless islands, the very essence of a tropical paradise.

Among these, only three nautical miles from San Pedro harbor, is Cayo Espanto, a resort that could serve as a private island for your honeymoon. It has only seven wooden villas, each with its own beach and jetty, and in which you can stay as if the rest of the world doesn't exist. Pampered by service that is simply... *unbelizeable*!

Paradise Island

Bahamas

242 / 243 - Consisting of 365 islands and islets with white sand that dot the ocean for over 118 miles, Exuma is one of the loveliest archipelagos in the Bahamas. This paradise has served as the setting for several James Bond movies.

When he was asked what he thought was the most beautiful place on earth as he looked down from a porthole of the International Space Station, the Canadian astronaut Chris Hadfield answered with no hesitation: "The most beautiful place from space is the Bahamas, with all the gorgeous colors of the ocean... The beauty of the Bahamas is surreal; every blue that exists."

Now, thanks to the technology of Google Earth, one needn't travel to space to have a view of that sea dotted with 700 islands (only 300 of which are inhabited); enthralled by what you see on your computer screen, you will be overcome a moment later by an urge to fly to one of these tiny paradises in order to experience the rewarding sense of freedom that only a tropical beach can offer.

To be sure, only the 'usual' happy few, including Hollywood stars and CEOs of billion-dollar multinational firms, can afford to purchase an entire island in the Bahamas; in any case, the luxury sector of the real estate market is becoming increasingly expensive. But you can content yourself, so to speak, with a vacation in the resorts

of the archipelago. And you needn't be too far away from New Providence, the island holding Nassau, the lively capital of the Bahamas, and the international airport, since a bridge connects it to another island the name of which is promising in itself: Paradise Island.

Considered the 'amusement park' of the archipelago, Paradise Island boasts many a record. No other island in the world has ever been the refuge, twice, for so-called Caribbean pirates, the first, real 18th-century ones (the notorious Henry Morgan, Calico Jack, and Blackbeard) and the fictional ones of the movies (the equally famous Johnny Depp). Furthermore, no other island has served as the location of four James Bond movies. Underwater combats as well as passionate underwater love scenes have been shot in its crystal clear waters – in *Thunderball*, *The Spy Who Loved Me* and *Never Say Never Again* – while in the more recent *Casino Royale*, Daniel Craig does an acrobatic parking stint with his Aston Martin DB5 before the One&Only Ocean Club, the most exclusive resort in the Bahamas.

As they say, it is better not to repeat James Bond's exploits. Leaving aside expert automobile maneuvers, this resort invites you to enjoy more romantic pleasures, such as relaxing on dreamy beaches with sand as white as sugar, gourmet dinners, and walks in a huge garden modeled upon the one at Versailles but reinterpreted in a sensuous 'tropical' key. Indeed, the estate even has a 12th-century Augustinian cloister transported from France and reassembled piece by piece – a magnificent location for the frequent wedding ceremonies performed here. Other fantastic experiences in store for couples throughout the island include snorkeling and diving on the reef, swimming together with dolphins at Dolphin Cay, and wonderful excursions in a catamaran. Alternatively you can spend your time people-watching, checking out celebrities. The habitués of Paradise Island include Beyoncé, Alicia Keys, and the utterly romantic Michael Bublé.

244 - Paradise Island Light is the icon of Nassau Harbor. Built in 1816, it is the oldest still operative lighthouse in the West Indies. One can get there on foot by starting off from splendid Coral Beach.

245 *top* - Designed by Tom Weiskopf, the legendary golf course architect of the PGA Tour, the Ocean Club is one of the most prestigious courses in the Caribbean.

245 *bottom* - Luxurious and romantic Ocean Club Resort even has a 12th-century Augustinian cloister, transported from France and reassembled here, which overlooks a garden laid out along the lines of the one at Versailles.

Montego Bay
Jamaica

246 - Doctor's Cave Beach is the best-known beach in Jamaica. It was named after a late 19th-century British osteopath who prescribed bathing in this sea for its beneficial effect on bones. What is certain is that a vacation on this island is a remedy for stress, allowing one to enjoy the wonderful beaches of Montego Bay, reggae music, as well as the beautiful scenery of the interior, first and foremost famous Ocho Rios Falls.

247 - The spa at the legendary Round Hill Resort lies in a converted 18th-century colonial plantation mansion overlooking a large lawn and the sea.

"I wanna love you and treat you right; / I wanna love you every day and every night; / We'll be together with a roof right over our heads; / We'll share the shelter of my single bed." This is the beginning of Bob Marley's *Is This Love?* – perhaps his most romantic song. Upon hearing it, you immediately have the urge to embrace your beloved or find someone to love, to dance with, and then take him or her to a simple place with a thatched roof – a warm place in Jamaica. Thanks to Bob Marley, you can already imagine yourself in Jamaica, a mythical island for over a generation (even among young people, who know it as the island of the great sprinter Usain Bolt). You can feel it inside yourself, though you haven't even been there yet.

Jamaicans say that those who want sun, beaches, and palm trees should go to St. Bath or some other place in the Caribbean. According to them, the country is in the Caribbean Islands solely by geographical error, so to speak, for its heart is really African. People come to it to live, intensely, very intensely. Jamaica has all that the rest of the Caribbean has – a dream sea, beaches, palm trees and a sort of vacation-like hedonism that puts you in a good mood – but it also has much more. Like the Rastafarian heritage of Bob Marley, which you can experience in the capital, Kingston, and in Negril, in legendary Rick's Cafe, which clings to the tip of West End Cliff, where people dance all day and night to the beat of reggae. You must also discover the interior of the island, from the Blue Mountains, where the most highly prized coffee in the world is grown, to the tropical forest of Ocho Rios, traversed by rivers on which

you can go rafting on bamboo rafts and enjoy a romantic swim amongst waterfalls. You can also explore the island's coastal grottoes, which, according to legend, still contain buried pirate treasure. Or you can visit splendid Victorian and Georgian colonial houses, but with caution, for some swear that Rose Hall House, the most grandiose of all, is haunted by the ghost of its owner, Annie Palmer. Known on the island as the White Witch, Palmer lived on this estate in the 19th century. Local legend has it that she controlled the many slaves on her plantation as well as her various husbands and lovers with an iron fist. On the west coast, Montego Bay is the pearl of Jamaican vacations and too has much to offer. The American movie star Errol Flynn, who made the place famous, arrived here in 1942 and declared: "It's more beautiful than any woman I have ever known." Flynn became a habitué of Round Hill, the marvelous colonial style resort that has since been restored with the utmost care, along with its interior, by the fashion designer Ralph Lauren (now a member of the owners' board) and which lies at the very heart of the so-called hip strip, the most lively beach on Montego Bay. Playwright Noël Coward lived and wrote in one of its villas, and many other VIPS have likewise spent vacations here: British aristocrats, heads of state (JFK several times with Jackie), Hollywood celebrities, and rock stars. So, in order to make your Jamaican dream come true, be sure to reserve the cottage that was the love nest of Marilyn Monroe and Arthur Miller, and who came here on their honeymoon. If you don't believe this, there is a lovely photograph of them on the walls of the restaurant.

The Lesser Antilles

Barbados, Trinidad & Tobago, Grenada, St. Vincent and the Grenadines, Guadeloupe, Dominica, St. Lucia

One part West Indian lime, two parts sugar syrup, three parts rum, and four of crushed ice: this is the recipe for rum punch, the *cocktail* of Barbados. For that matter, the basic ingredient was invented on this island, which has the world's oldest commercial rum distillery, Mount Gay, founded by the British in 1703. They say here that in order to really enjoy this drink you must add another ingredient: a beach, any beach, since there are about 100 along the coastline of the easternmost island of the Lesser Antilles, one more beautiful than the next. British sailors supposedly invented this medicinal cocktail 400 years ago: the lime cured scurvy, a common disease among sailors at the time, while the liquor that the natives distilled from sugar cane was a remedy for homesickness.

Today we dare anyone who sips this drink while sitting on a beach in Barbados – the most sophisticated and British of the Caribbean islands – to wish to return home. If anything, he or she will stare at the horizon and dream of weighing anchor

to begin an adventure on the open blue sea. There is no better harbor to embark on an old-fashioned cruise than Bridgetown, the delightful capital, with its monument to Horatio Nelson, one of history's most famous admirals. Offering this exciting experience is the *Sea Cloud*, a legendary four-mast schooner with trapezoidal sails (the technical name for which is windjammer) launched in 1931. You can reserve one of its 32 elegant cabins with a king-size bed and antique furniture, or you can rent the entire vessel with the person dearest to you in order to celebrate a special occasion. Whatever the case, the *Sea Cloud* will sail on a ten-day circular tour that includes some of the most extraordinary destinations in the Lesser Antilles, hours and hours of navigation in truly grand style.

Every day a new thrill awaits you, from a dive into enchanting Man O'War Bay in Tobago or Chatham Bay on Union Island in the Grenadines, to an excursion to nutmeg-, cinnamon-, clove- and ginger-scented gardens in St. George, the capital

248 / 249 - Even in Tobago's marvelous Union Island Bay, which is always full of luxury yachts, a boat such as *Sea Cloud* stands out among the rest. This 359-ft. long legendary windjammer with four masts and 30 trapezoidal sails was built in the shipyard of Kiel, Germany, for a rich Wall Street broker in 1931.

of the island of Grenada. You can explore the forest of Cabrits on the island of Dominica and indulge in the French atmosphere of the tiny archipelago of the Îles des Saintes, in Guadeloupe. Then comes time for the beaches and panoramic views from the tall volcanic craters of St. Lucia, where, in an idyllic tropical park, you can swim in the sulfuric hot springs once frequented by Joséphine de Beauharnais, the Caribbean beauty and Napoleon's first, beloved wife. What's more, you can observe from up close the sea turtles of Margaret Beach, the splendid nature reserve on Bequia, the second largest in the Grenadine Islands. Finally, as you return to Barbados you can raise your glass of rum punch and toast what will have been a great romantic adventure and a true test of love. For every day on a sailboat with your partner is worth a year spent together on the mainland. Take a sea dog's word for it.

250 - It is not easy to choose the 'right' beach in Barbados as there are 100 of them, all beautiful. The Caribbean has thrills in store even under water.

251 - The *Sea Cloud* is absolutely charming, from its teakwood decks and shiny brass fittings to its communal areas and impressive large cabins. The most luxurious cabin is the one that Marjorie Merriweather Post, the first owner of this sailboat, chose for herself, fitting it out with authentic Louis XIV furniture and brocade. And let's not forget the elegant white Carrara marble fireplace.

The Talamanca Mountains
Costa Rica

252 *top* - Although a large population of jaguars lives on the slopes of Talamanca Mountains, this creature is very reclusive and difficult to spot.

252 *bottom* - It is not hard to understand why this suite in Pacuare Lodge has been named Linda Vista (beautiful view), given the luxurious hospitality offered at this resort, which is situated in one of the most pristine areas of Central America.

253 - The Pacuare River originates in Talamanca Mountains and is a sort of meeting point for flora and fauna species of North and South America.

Over 60 years ago this country decided to do without an army and spend its money not on armaments but rather on preserving and defending what it considers most precious, its nature, which is truly exceptional. Situated between Panama and Nicaragua and bordered on one side by the Pacific and the other by the Caribbean, Costa Rica occupies a mere 0.03% of the land on our planet but is home to 5% of its biodiversity. In terms of environmental protection, it is one of the five leading countries in the world. Suffice it to say that the year 2000 marked the birth of Nature Air, the first eco-friendly airline, which uses biodiesel fuel for its airplanes, then calculates the amount of carbon emission caused by its flights each year and donates a corresponding amount of money to finance nature conservation. So, for those concerned with ethical questions, Costa Rica is the place to go for a zero-impact vacation, during which you can enjoy nature, experience the thrill of adventure and even live in what could be called eco-luxury. And while it comes as no surprise that exclusive resorts exist near and in its capital, San José, and along its coasts, what is truly interesting is that you can have 'sophisticated' adventures even in its most remote areas. Among these, mention must be made of the Talamanca Mountains – inhabited by scattered communities of Cabecar Indians and surrounded by impenetrable rain forests, among the last habitats of jaguars, and thus a marvelous Latin American

version of a 'heart of darkness.' Immersed – there is no better word to describe this – in such a primeval setting, is the extraordinary Pacuare Lodge, named after the river that affords the only access to this paradise. Indeed, you must undertake a true rafting adventure to get there, struggling with the impetuous flow of water through a tunnel of vegetation, with the calls of tropical birds as the 'sound track' of your expedition. Upon arrival you will be ushered into one of the very chic bungalows built among trees. Should you decide to reserve a honeymoon suite, you will even get a private pool overlooking the jungle. Your stay here will be unforgettable as you trek on foot or horseback, go on bird-watching expeditions, pay visits to native communities and take canopy tours – an 'adrenaline activity' that enables you to experience rainforest life from the viewpoint of… Tarzan and Jane, rappelling nearly 32 yards above ground and swinging as far as 765 yards, from one wooden platform to another among the tree tops. Speaking of 'aerial experiences,' the Pacuare Lodge offers a very special one, El Nido, a wooden platform with a palm leaf roof 22 yards above ground, which in the evening becomes a restaurant for two where you can enjoy a romantic dinner in the wild. Be warned, however, that the lodge has no telephones, Internet connection, or television (except for free WIFI in the reception area). But then, so what? After such a fascinating dinner they would only be a nuisance, wouldn't they?

The Amazon Rainforest
Ecuador

The main obstacle here is to convince her that no, both of you will not have your blood sucked by mosquitoes, be poisoned by a monstrous spider, crushed by an anaconda or devoured by piranhas. You will tell her that yes, it's true that there is an entire series of Hollywood movies based on adventures in Amazonia that end tragically, but in reality the possibility of triggering the fury of these 'murderous animals' is extremely remote. What you ought to tell her is that there is no better gift for demonstrating love than a trip to this green paradise, the largest and thickest forest on earth.

Precisely because of its almost inconceivable size, a trip to the Amazon Rainforest should be planned with great care. While most of the forest lies in Brazil – and along the course of the Amazon River, which flows for more than 3728 miles, taking in the waters of 10,000 tributaries – other countries provide easier access to its dark heart and have tourist facilities that offer extraordinary wild adventures with style and precisely the right amount of a romantic atmosphere. Among these, first place goes to Ecuador, given that it takes only

30 minutes by airplane, plus a couple of hours in a motorized canoe, to get from the capital Quito to one of the most amazing corners of the rain forest. An intelligent choice is the intriguing 'honeymoon package' (which includes, among other things, dinners by candlelight and massages at the spa) at La Selva Amazon Ecolodge, situated at the edge of fabulous Yasuni National Park and offering guests 12 super-luxury suites constructed of ecologically compatible materials. The park, lying between the Napo and Cuary Rivers, has a total surface area of only 38.6 square miles (0.15 % of the Amazon Rain Forest) but is considered by some to be the place with the greatest amount of biodiversity in the world.

Make sure that your partner learns certain data about the park only after arrival; if possible, have one of the excellent nature guides at the lodge provide this information. Indeed, Yasuni Park holds the record, in proportion to its size, for the number of amphibian (150), reptile (120), fish (382) and insect (100,000) species, and is home to 586 species of birds, one-third of the total number in

254 / 255 - Occupying barely 0.15 per cent of the Amazon Rainforest, Yasuni National Park is considered the world's most bio-diverse area. Here one can come across extraordinary animals such as the elegant ocelot, as well as primitive Amerindian tribes. Among the latter are the Huaorani, who still hunt with blowpipes.

the entire Amazon basin. It also has large communities of monkeys and groups of armadillos, tapirs and jaguars. As for its flora, there is no other park on earth with so many species of tall trees and lianas. What is perhaps even more surprising, in addition to the friendly Huaorani and Kichwa populations, the park is home to two indigenous hunter-gatherer ethnic groups, the Tagaeri and Taromenan, both of which belong among the ever decreasing number of so-called uncontacted tribes.

La Selva Ecolodge organizes adventures for discovering the inestimable natural treasures of the forest. Only a few hundred yards from it lies the so-called Napo River parrot clay lick, the best place in Ecuador – and in all of Amazonia – for bird watching. And only a short walk away is a very romantic butterfly sanctuary.

256 - Built with bamboo grown on eco-sustainable plantations and in a style that recreates a forest atmosphere, La Selva Amazon Ecolodge & Spa lies in a marvelous position overlooking Lake Garzacocha.

257 *top* - La Selva Ecclodge is in one of the most incredible areas in all of Amazonia. Simply getting there is an adventure. From Quito, the capital of Ecuador, guests take a half-hour flight on a small plane to the town of Coca, and from there a two-and-a-half hour ride on a motorized canoe along Rio Napo.

257 *bottom* - A must is a walk in the company of a local guide and lodge naturalist through Yasuni National Park to see the area's gigantic trees.

From Cuzco to Machu Picchu
Peru

258 - Situated at an altitude of 7972 feet over the Urubamba River, Machu Picchu is one of the most spectacular and mysterious archeological sites in the world. It is the climax of any vacation in Peru, together naturally with the Inca city of Cuzco, where the best place to stay is historic La Casona Hotel, located in a Spanish colonial building that housed the troops of the bloodthirsty conquistador, Francisco Pizarro.

259 - A young Quechua Indios with his young alpaca posing before the walls of impressive Sacsayhuamán, the Inca fortress in Cuzco.

Inca is a name that exudes mystery. In Quechua, the language spoken by the main ethnic group in Peru, it means 'prince,' a demigod and supreme ruler of a nation that believed itself to be at the center of the universe. And Cuzco, the name of its capital, means 'navel' (of the world). The Inca appellation for sovereign became the collective name of the people who, in the 13th century, began to rule as one of the largest, best organized and most powerful empires in human history over all other populations in the Peruvian Andes, eventually dominating – from the Qurikancha, the temple-fortress of Cuzco whose walls were once covered with gold and precious stones – a vast area in South America for over a century. Given all this, it is nothing less than incredible that in 1531 this empire was defeated by a small group of Spaniards led by the treacherous Francisco Pizarro, who betrayed and killed Atahualpa, its ruling prince.

In order to find yourself at the very heart of the mysterious and highly fascinating history of the Incas, you should stay at the La Casona hotel, situated in the very building in Cuzco that Pizarro built as lodgings for his troops. Nowadays, needless to say, the atmosphere has hardly anything martial about it, but instead holds a seductive mixture of Spanish antique furnishings, superb Quechuan handicrafts, and precious Baroque paintings of the so-called Esquela Cusqueña, the most sophisticated artistic school of colonial America. In short, this hotel consists of layers of cultures, as does this extraordinary Andean city 11,151 feet above sea level, which bewitches visitors with its plazas, incredibly ornate churches – especially La Compañía, La Merced and the Cathedral of Santo Domingo, built over the foundations of the above-mentioned Qurikancha temple – and its inhabitants, proud Indios dressed in colorful ponchos whose facial features reveal that they are descendents of Prince Atahualpa. In Cuzco, it is a special treat to lose your way among the narrow alleyways of San Blás, the artisans' quarter, and to greet the setting sun in the thin and transparent air while sitting on the terraces of a café, or perhaps to try the typical mate de coca, the herbal coca tea that is the best remedy for altitude sickness. Following the tracks of Quechuan tales and legends, you must head from Cuzco to the Sacred Valley of the Incas, a walk of about 25 miles (a two-day trip) that passes through corn fields and old Andean villages, each with its own multicolored market. At the end of the second day you will arrive at Aguasacalientes, a town overlooking the Urubamba River, which, with its atmosphere of a festive moving celebration, heralds a marvelous reward for this fatiguing walk: Machu Picchu, the Lost City of the Incas. Your final effort should be to arrive there at dawn, when the first rays of the sun disperse the fog, revealing the stunning spectacle of one of the most captivating and mysterious archeological sites on earth.

Trancoso
Brazil

Very few people know that the *descubrimiento* – the term for the discovery of Brazil by Portuguese navigators – did not take place on or near famous Copacabana beach or in a bay or cove in equally renowned Bahia, but in a place halfway between these two. To be more precise, 497 miles from one and 497 miles from the other. On 22 April 1500, the person who shouted "Land ahoy!" was Pedro Alvarez Cabral, who had spotted a strip of white sand with a mass of tropical forest looming behind it. To his left, in the distance, he caught sight of a mountain; since this occurred on Easter Sunday, Cabral called it Monte Pascoal (Mt. Easter) despite the fact that it had the shape of a traditional Christmas cake. The landing point, on the other hand, was christened – as a good omen – Porto Seguro or 'safe port.' Later, in 1586, a group of Jesuits (utterly unlike other more determined missionaries) chose a level area about 18 miles from that landing place, on which they founded a church and built 50 small houses, imagining that the Indios would live there in harmony with God and nature. That village, formally named São João Batista dos Indios, came to be called Trancoso by the local people. Considered the Bali of South America, Trancoso is now the most romantic seaside destination in Brazil. But, unlike Bali, it has managed to put a check on mass tourism. In fact your arrival there – along a road with numerous holes and almost totally covered by the forest that connects Trancoso to Porto Seguro – will still have the flavor of a *descubrimiento*. Called the Quadrado, the green square bordered by the old church (which is extremely popular as a wedding venue) and colonial houses seems to be a genuine utopia. Leaving aside the permanent residents – a handful of Indios and mestizos who survive by fishing and agriculture, a group of artists who have abandoned Rio de Janeiro and São Paulo, and a policeman sent there as part of the decor, since there is no crime – visitors in Trancoso have no large hotels at their disposal but must content themselves with a few glamorous, very chic, colorful tropical-style *pousadas* or inns. Among these, the most 'in' is the Uxua, which offers charming houses amid a luxuriant garden and a spa with the only pool in the world faced with thousands of pieces of aventurine, a very special quartz that seems to act as a powerful catalyst of positive energy.

260 / 261 - Only a few minutes' walk from fascinating Quadrado Square in the heart of Trancoso, Uxua Beach is part of Uxua Casa Hotel and Spa, the chicest ones in the village. In the state of Bahia, precisely halfway between Salvador and Rio de Janeiro, Trancoso is somewhat 'neo-hippy' (and very much in vogue) and has wonderful beaches, such as Praia do Espelho.

The Atacama Desert
Chile

262 - Alto Atacama Desert Lodge & Spa was built in adobe, modeled after a typical Andean village but with the addition of a great deal of luxury. A short distance from here – and from the town of San Pedro de Atacama – are sites such as extraordinary Laguna Miscanti in Los Flamencos National Reserve.

263 - With a surface area of 1158 square miles and lying 7752 feet above sea level, the salt flat known as Salar de Atacama is a phenomenal site with surreal scenery that seems to belong to the planet Mars. Surprisingly, it is also economically rich as it possesses the world's richest lithium deposits.

It was here that NASA tested the Viking I and II probes before sending them off to Mars, because this desert, where rainfall worthy of the name has never been recorded throughout the history of mankind and where the riverbeds have not had a drop of rain in 120,000 years, is the area on Earth most similar to the terrain of the Red Planet. You will see what can only be called outer space sunsets in the Valley of the Moon, thus named due to its alien scenery, so remote from the one that we know and so similar to that of our satellite. Here, at an altitude ranging from 6562 to 19,685 feet, the air is extremely thin and it takes a bit of time to adapt to, while the sky is so clear – thanks to the absence of light pollution and humidity – that astronomers come to observe the stars, which seem much closer than anywhere else on the planet. Incredibly enough, an Andean civilization flourished here in the Paleolithic period; in fact the Atacama Desert is the archeological treasure of Chile. In San Pedro de Atacama, a town of a little more than 2000 souls, which serves as its capital, there is even a museum.

Defining this desert as arid is a euphemism, but considering such an arid, unworldly place as a destination only for tough people (or space and astronomy buffs) would be a serious mistake. An 'extreme vacation' – and it would be hard to find a place more extreme than this one – could be a test of love, a Technicolor anticipation of the inevitable difficulties and immense joys of life. And, as far as joy is concerned, there is an abundance of it here: incredibly beautiful landscapes that unfold like mirages at the end of a canyon or beyond the crest of a mountain. It is simply thrilling, for example, to arrive in Salar de Atacama, the third largest salt flat in the world, where you can (finally) see a very thin sheet of water dotted with formations of salt crystals similar to mushrooms, as well as thousands of pink flamingoes along with lizards and llamas, the only animals that have managed to adapt to the life there. The Atacama Desert also has dozens of trekking trails that can be negotiated on foot, horseback or bicycle and that lead to prodigious natural phenomena, including rock formations of a surreal gamut of colors and very tall geysers.

Among its many delights, Atacama Desert also offers an apparently incongruous experiences of extreme luxury, as in the exceptional Alto Atacama Desert Lodge & Spa, which lies in an enchanting basin among craggy, sharp red rocks and constructed in a minimalist chic style, with no fewer than 6 swimming pools (a paradox, given the absolute lack of water in the area) and a private observatory. In short, this lodge is a refuge where you can really touch the sky.

El Calafate
Argentina

264 - A few hours of relaxation in the splendid pool (facing Lake Argentino) of elegant and ultramodern El Calafate Design Suites is just what the doctor ordered before embarking on an adventurous trip to Perito Moreno Glacier, the 'superstar' of Argentine Patagonia. The glacier extends over an area of 96 square miles and is the third largest freshwater reserve in the world.

265 - The light of dawn lends a golden hue to Mt. Fitz Roy, also known as Cerro Chaltén. The name given it by the Mapuche Indios means 'smoking mountain' due to the clouds that often envelop its summit.

As the Argentinians themselves say, what they do best is create myths. Think of the tango, Evita Perón, and, above all, *the* romantic hero of modern times, Ernesto Che Guevara. As handsome as they come and with adventure in his blood, – Che made the most insane trip on earth, down Ruta (National Route) 40 long before he met Fidel Castro and became part of his revolution. This too is an Argentine myth, as it traverses the entire western length of the country for around 3107 miles, from the tropical setting of the Argentine-Bolivian border to the tip of Argentina and Chile, at the ice caps of Patagonia. Don't worry, we are not recommending that you relive Che's feat (which he achieved mostly on a motorcycle), but merely consider the idea of going to the most mythical area in Argentina, Patagonia, on Ruta 40, or more precisely, on the stretch that connects Bariloche and El Calafate.

The surface of the road is not the most comfortable, to put it mildly. But the road winds through solitary countryside, along endless and dramatically beautiful pasture. When from the distance you spot the profile of Mt. Fitz Roy, the supreme mountaineering icon, you will know you are approaching your destination. The last stretch of road between El Chaltén, the frontier town that serves as the base for climbs up this famous mountain, and El Calafate will be a thrilling anticipation of the most stunning scenery in Patagonia:

the 1,101,843-acre Los Glaciares National Park, with 47 glaciers, plus many lakes and mountains.

Founded as recently as 1927 on the southern bank of Lake Argentino, the largest body of water in the country, El Calafate is the principal gateway to the national park and is a delightful tourist sight where you can be pampered after the fatigue of your long trip, in a dream hotel, El Calafate Design Suites, which offers unexpected – and most welcome – contemporary chic luxury. A night here is what you need before an excursion to the Perito Moreno Glacier, whose amazing light blue tongues open a passage between the Canal de los Tímpanos and the main basin of the lake. During the summer, if you are lucky, you may be able to observe a remarkable spectacle of blocks of ice that, due to a rise in water level causes them to crack, break off from the glacier and collapse into the lake with a thunderous roar.

If, on the other hand, you are unable to witness the above, you may have another opportunity to do so. El Calafate was named after the barberry or calafate, which is very similar in color and taste to the huckleberry and grows on thorny bushes only in this area. And according to a Tehuelche Indian legend, whoever eats these berries will surely return to Patagonia. So, go gather some during a romantic walk along the shores of this lake, or order the juice at the hotel. Perhaps accompanied by ice cream.

AUTHOR

JASMINA TRIFONI is a journalist specializing in tourism. She worked at the *Meridiani* magazine for ten years and now writes for leading Italian periodicals in this sector.

For White Star Publishers she has written *The Treasures of Art, Nature Sanctuaries and Ancient Civilizations* in the *The World Heritage Sites of UNESCO* series, *The Great Cities of the World, 80 Islands to Escape to... and Live Happily Ever After, The World's 100 Best Adventure Trips*, as well as *Dream Vacations* for the Cube Book series.

RESORT

Bora Bora - French Polynesia
Four Seasons Resort Bora Bora, Motu Tehotu,
Bora Bora, Tel. +689 603130,
www.fourseasons.com/borabora

Vanua Levu - Fiji
Jean-Michel Cousteau Resort, Savusavu, Vanua Levu,
Tel. +1 415 7885794, www.fijiresort.com

Vava'u - Tonga
The Moorings, Tel. +64 9 3787900,
www.tongasailing.com

Kaua'i - USA
St Regis Princeville, 5520 Ka Haku Road,
Princeville, Kaua'i, Tel. +1 808 8269644,
www.stregisprinceville.com

The Blue Mountains - Australia
Emirates Wolgan Valley Resort & Spa,
2600 Wolgan Road, Wolgan Valley, Lithgow,
Tel. +61 2 63501800, www.wolganvalley.com

Ayers Rock - Australia
Longitude 131°, Yulara Drive, Yulara, NT,
Tel. +61 1300 134044, longitude131.com.au

Hamilton Island - Australia
Qualia Resort, 20 Whitsunday Boulevard, Hamilton
Island, Tel. +61 2 94333349, www.qualia.com.au

One&Only Hayman Island - Australia
One&Only Hayman Island, Great Barrier Reef,
Queensland 4801, tel. +61 7 49401234,
www.hayman.oneandonlyresorts.com

Lake Taupo - New Zealand
Huka Lodge, Huka Falls Road, Taupo,
Tel. +64 7 3785791, www.hukalodge.co.nz

Queenstown - New Zealand
Matakauri Lodge, Farrycroft Row, 569 Glenorchy
Road, Queenstown, Tel. +64 3 4411008,
www.matakauri.co.nz

Bali - Indonesia
Alila Villas Soori, Banjar Dukuh, Desa Kelating,
Kerambitan, Tabanan, Tel. +62 361 8946388,
www.alilahotels.com/soori

Kyoto - Japan
Hiiragiya Ryokan, Nakahakusancho, Fuyacho
Anekoji-agaru, Nakagyo-ku,
Tel. +81 75 2211139, www.hiiragiya.co.jp

Hangzhou - China
Fuchun Resort, Fuyang Section, 339 Jiangbin
Dongdadao, Dongzhou Area, Hangzhou,
Tel. +86 571 6346 1111, www.fuchunresort.com/en

Yunnan Province - China
Banyan Tree Lijiang, Yuerong Road, Shuhe Gucheng
District, Lijiang, Tel. +86 888 5331111,
www.banyantree.com/en/lijiang

In the Valleys of Bhutan - Bhutan
Uma by Como, PO Box 222, Paro, Bhutan,
Tel. +975 271597,
www.amanresorts.com/amankora/home.aspx

Hoi An - Vietnam
The Nam Hai, Hamlet 1, Dien Duong Village,
Dien Ban District, Quang Nam Province
Tel. +84 510 3940000,
www.ghmhotels.com/en/nam-hai

Luang Prabang - Laos
Belmond La Résidence Phou Vao, Luang Prabang,
Tel. +856 71 212530, www.belmond.com

Angkor - Cambodia
Raffles Grand Hotel d'Angkor, 1 Vithei Charles
de Gaulle, Khum Svay Dang Kum, Siem Reap,
Tel. +855 63 963888, www.raffles.com/siemreap

Krabi - Thailand
Rayavadee, 214 Moo 2, Tambon Ao-Nang,
Amphoe Muang, Krabi, Tel. +66 75 620740 a 3,
www.rayavadee.com

Chiang Mai - Thailand
Dhara Dhevi, 51/4 Chiang Mai-Sankampaeng Road,
Moo 1, T. Tasala, A. Muang, Chiang Mai,
Tel. +66 53 888888, www.dharadhevi.com

Along the Irrawaddy - Myanmar
Belmond Road to Mandalay,
Tel. +44 20 31171300, www.belmond.com

Agra - India
The Oberoi Amarvilas, Agra,
Tel. +91 562 2231515,
www.oberoihotels.com/oberoi_amarvilas

Jaipur - India
Rambagh Palace, Bhawani Singh Rd, Rambagh,
Jaipur, Tel. +91 141 2211919, www.tajhotels.com/
Luxury/Grand-Palaces-And-Iconic-Hotels/Rambagh-
Palace-Jaipur/Overview.html

Galle - Sri Lanka
Kahanda Kanda, Angulugaha, Galle,
Tel. +94 91 4943700, www.kahandakanda.com

The Maldive Islands - Republic of the Maldives
Four Seasons Resort Maldives at Landaa Giraavaru,
Tel. +960 6600888,
www.fourseasons.com/maldiveslg

Dubai - United Arab Emirates
One&Only Royal Mirage, Al Sufouh Road, Jumeirah,
Dubai, Tel. +971 4 3999999, royalmirage.
oneandonlyresorts.com

Petra - Jordan
Evason Ma'In Hot Springs, Six Senses Resort & Spa,
Ma'in, Madaba, Tel. +962 5 3245500,
www.sixsenses.com/evason-resorts/ma-in/destination

The Turkish Coast - Turkey
Exclusive Gulets (www.exclusivegulets.co.uk)

Lapland - Sweden
Ice Hotel, Jukkasjärvi, Tel. +46 980 66800,
www.icehotel.com

Saint Petersburg - Russia
Hotel Astoria, 41 Bolshaya Morskaya,
St. Petersburg, Tel. +7 4 4945757,
www.roccofortehotels.com/hotels-and-resorts/hotel-
astoria

The Sunnmøre Alps - Norway
Juvet Landscape Hotel, Alstad, Valldal, Korcula,
Tel. +47 950 32010, www.juvet.com

The Scottish Highlands - United Kingdom
Ardanaiseig Hotel, Kilchrenan by Taynuilt, Argyll,
Tel. +44 1866 988205, www.ardanaiseig.com,
hello@ardanaiseig.com

Saint-Malo - France
Château de Colombier, Petit Paramé, Saint-Malo,
Tel. +32 2 23520228,
www.saintmalo-hotelcolombier.com

Champagne - France
Domaine Les Crayères, 64 Boulevard Henri Vasnier,
Reims, Tel. +33 3 26249000, www.lescrayeres.com

The Loire Valley - France
Château des Briottières, Route de Marigné,
Champigné, Tel. +33 241 420002,
www.briottieres.com

Die Romantische Strasse - Germany
Das König Ludwig Hotel, Spa & Wellness, Kreuzweg
15, Schwangau, Tel. +49 8362 8890,
www.koenig-ludwig-hoTel.de

St Moritz - Switzerland
The Chedi Andermatt, Gotthardstrasse 4,
Andermatt, Tel. +41 41 418887488,
www.ghmhotels.com/en/the-chedi-andermatt

Megève - France
Les Fermes de Marie, 163 Chemin de Riante Colline,
Mègeve, Tel. +33 4 50930310,
www.fermesdemarie.com

Cortina d'Ampezzo - Italy
Cristallo Hotel, Spa & Golf, via R. Menardi 42,
Cortina d'Ampezzo, Tel. +41 0436 881111,
www.cristallo.it

Venice - Italy
Hotel Danieli, Riva degli Schiavoni 4196, Venezia,
Tel. +41 041 5226480, www.danielihotelvenice.com

Verona - Italy
Byblos Art Hotel Villa Amistà, via Cedrare 78,
Corrubbio Verona, Tel. +41 045 6855555,
www.raffles.com/siemreap

Portofino - Italy
Belmond Hotel Splendido e Splendido Mare, Salita
Baratta 16, Portofino, Tel. +41 0185 267800, www.
hotelsplendido.com

Côte d'Azur - France
La Colombe d'Or, Place du Général De Gaulle,
Saint-Paul-de-Vence, Tel. +33 4 93328002,
www.la-colombe-dor.com

The Tuscan Hills - Italy
Relais La Suvera, via della Suvera 70, Pievescola,
Casole d'Elsa, Tel. +41 0577 960300,
www.lasuvera.it

The Amalfi Coast - Italy
Belmond Hotel Caruso, piazza San Giovanni del Toro 2,
Ravello, Tel. +41 089 858800,
www.hotelcaruso.com

Korčula - Croatia
Lešic Dimitri Palace, Don Pavla Poše 1-6, Korcula,
Tel. +385 20 715560, www.lesic-dimitri.com

Santorini - Greece
Mystique Resort, Oia, Santorini,
Tel. +30 228 6071114, www.mystique.gr

Andalusia - Spain
Hotel Alfonso XIII, Calle San Fernando 2, Siviglia,
Tel. +34 95 4917000,
www.hotel-alfonsoxiii-seville.com

The Douro Valley - Portugal
Aquapura Douro Valley, Quinta de Vale Abraão,
Samodães, Lamego, Tel. +351 254 660600,
www.aquapurahotels.com

The Azores - Portugal
Aldeia da Cuada, Faja Grande, 9960-070 Lajes
Das Flores, Tel. +351 292 590040,
www.wonderfulland.com/cuada

Marrakech - Morocco
Ksar Char-Bagh, La Palmeraie, Marrakech,
Tel. +212 524 329244, www.ksarcharbagh.com

Along the Nile - Egypt
Nour el Nil, reservations Tel. +20 1 05705341,
www.nourelnil.com, info@nourelnil.com

Seychelles - Republic of Seychelles
Frégate Island Private, Victoria, Mahé Republic of
Seychelles Tel. +248 4 670100, www.fregate.
com. Frégate Island Private is a resort in the Oetker
Collection, which is comprised of 8 masterpiece hotels
throughout the world (www.oetkercollection.com)

The Masai Mara - Kenya
Cottar's 1920s Camp, Cottar's Private Conservancy,
Olderikesi, South East Maasai Mara,
Tel. +254 733 773378, www.cottars.com

Serengeti - Tanzania
Singita Serengeti, Tel. +27 21 6833424,
www.singita.com, enquiries@singita.com

Nosy Be - Madagascar
Constance Tsarabanjina Resort, B.P. 380,
Hel-Ville 207, Nosy Be, Tel. +261 32 0215229,
tsarabanjina.constancehotels.com

Mauritius - Republic of Mauritius
Le Touessrok, Flaq, Mauritius,
Tel. +230 4027400, www.letouessrokresort.com

Victoria Falls - Zambia/Zimbabwe
Royal Livingstone Hotel, Mosi-oa-Tunya Road,
Livingstone, Tel. +260 21 3321122,
www.suninternational.com/fallsresort/royal-
livingstone/Pages/default.aspx

The Moremi Game Reserve - Botswana
Little Mombo Camp, Moremi Natural Reserve,
reservations Tel. +27 11 8071800,
www.wilderness-safaris.com/camps/little-mombo

Kruger National Park - South Africa
Sabi Sabi Private Game Reserve, Kruger National
Park, Te. +27 11 4477172, www.sabisabi.com

The Namib Desert - Namibia
Dunes Lodge (Wolwedans Collection), NamibRand
Nature Reserve, Tel. +264 61 230616,
www.wolwedans.com

Whistler - Canada
Nita Lake Lodge, 2131 Lake Placid Road, Whistler,
BC, Tel. +1 604 9665700,
www.nitalakelodge.com

In Montana - USA
The Resort at Paws Up, 40060 Paws Up Road,
Greenough, Tel. +1 406 2445200,
www.pawsup.com

Nantucket and Martha's Vineyard - USA
The Wauwinet, 120 Wauwinet Road, Nantucket, MA,
Tel. +1 508 2280145,
www.wauwinet.com

San Francisco - USA
Cavallo Point – The Lodge at the Golden Gate,
601 Murray Circle, Fort Baker, Sausalito,
Tel. +1 415 3394700, www.cavallopoint.com

Moab - USA
Moab Under Canvas, 13784 North Highway 191,
Moab, Tel. +1 801 8953213,
www.moabundercanvas.com

Charleston - USA
Wentworth Mansion, 2149 Wentworth Street,
Charleston SC, Tel. +1 888 4661886,
www.wentworthmansion.com

The Florida Keys - USA
Little Palm Island Resort & Spa, 28500 Overseas
Highway, Little Torch Key, Tel. +1 305 8722524
www.littlepalmisland.com

Los Cabos - Mexico
Las Ventanas al Paraíso, km. 19.5 Ctra.
Transpeninsular, San Jose del Cabo,
Tel. +52 624 1442800,
www.rosewoodhotels.com/es/las-ventanas-los-cabos

San Miguel de Allende - Mexico
L'Ôtel San Miguel de Allende, Calle Ciquitos 1A,
Centro San Miguel de Allende 37700, Guanajuato,
Tel. +52 415 1549850,
www.l-otelgroup.com

Yucatán - Mexico
Hacienda Temozón, Km 182 Carretera Merida-Uxmal,
Temozón Sur, Yucatán, Tel. +52 999 9238089,
www.haciendatemozon.com

Ambergris Caye - Belize
A Private Island, Cayo Espanto,
Tel. +1 888 6664282, www.aprivateisland.com

Paradise Island - Bahamas
One&Only Ocean Club, One Casino Drive,
Paradise Island, Tel. +954 809 2150,
oceanclub.oneandonlyresorts.com

Montego Bay - Jamaica
Round Hill Hotel & Villas, John Pringle Drive,
Montego Bay, Tel. +1 876 9567050,
www.roundhill.com

**The Lesser Antilles - Barbados, Trinidad
& Tobago, Grenada, St. Vincent and
the Grenadines, Guadeloupe, Dominica,
St. Lucia**
Sea Cloud, Tel. +49 42 30959250,
www.seacloud.com

The Talamanca Mountains - Costa Rica
Pacuare Lodge, Pacuare Protegida Zone,
Turrialba, Tel. +506 2225 3939
www.pacuarelodge.com

The Amazon Rainforest - Ecuador
La Selva Amazon Ecolodge & Spa, Garzacoha,
Tel. +593 2 2540427,
www.laselvajunglelodge.com

From Cuzco to Machu Picchu - Peru
La Casona, Plazoleta Nazarenas 167, Cusco,
Tel. +51 1 6100400,
www.inkaterra.com/inkaterra/la-casona

Trancoso - Brazil
Uxua Casa Hotel & Spa, Quadrado, Trancoso, Bahia,
Tel. +55 73 3668 2277, uxua.com

The Atacama Desert - Chile
Alto Atacama Desert Lodge & Spa, Camino Pukará,
Sector Suchor, San Pedro de Atacama,
Tel. +56 2 9123945, www.altoatacama.com

El Calafate - Argentina
El Calafate Design Suites, Calle 598 NÂ°190, Playa
Lago Argentino, El Calafate, Santa Cruz,
Tel. +54 2902 494525,
www.designsuites.com/calafate

INDEX

PHOTOGRAPHIC CREDITS

Pages 2-3 Courtesy of the Singita Serengeti
Pages 8-9, 10 bottom, 11 top Courtesy of the Four Seasons Resort Bora Bora, Motu Tehotu
Page 10 top Michel Renaudeau/Age Fotostock
Page 12 Paul Nicklen/National Geographic Creative
Pages 12-13 Ethan Daniels/Age Fotostock
Page 14 Courtesy of the Chris McLennan/Jean Michel Cousteau Resort
Page 15 Radius Images/Corbis
Page 16 Galen Rowell/Corbis
Pages 17 top, 17 bottom Courtesy of the Chris McLennan/Jean Michel Cousteau Resort
Page 18 top Neil Rabinowitz/Corbis
Page 18 bottom Courtesy of the The Moorings
Page 19 Jason Isley - Scubazoo/Science Faction/Corbis
Page 20 Courtesy of the St Regis Princeville
Page 21 G. Sioen/De Agostini Picture Library
Pages 22 top, 22 bottom Courtesy of the Emirates Wolgan Valley Resort & Spa
Page 23 Steven J Taylor/Shutterstock
Pages 24 top, 24 bottom, 25, 26 top, 26 bottom, 27 top and bottom, Courtesy of the Longitude 131°
Page 28 top John Carnemolla/iStockphoto
Pages 28 bottom, 29 Courtesy of the qualia Resort
Pages 30, 31 Courtesy of the One&Only Hayman Island. Photographer Simon Upton
Pages 32, 35 bottom Courtesy of the Huka Lodge
Page 33 John Doornkamp/Design Pics/Corbis
Page 34 Woody Ang/Shutterstock
Page 35 top Michael Nolan/Robert Harding World Imagery/Corbis
Page 36 B Studio/Shutterstock
Pages 37 top, 37 bottom Courtesy of the Matakauri Lodge
Page 38 NCG/Shutterstock
Pages 38-39 Fakrul Jamil/Shutterstock
Page 40 Steve Rosenberg/Age Fotostock
Page 41 Knet2d/Age Fotostock
Page 42 McPHOTO/Age Fotostock
Page 43 top Sean White/Age Fotostock
Page 43 bottom Courtesy of the Alila Villas Soori
Page 44 top NH/Shutterstock
Page 44 bottom Courtesy of the Hiiragiya Ryokan
Page 45 cocozero003/123rf
Page 46 Courtesy of the Fuchun Resort
Page 47 chuyu/123rf
Page 48 ViewStock/View Stock RF/Age Fotostock
Page 49 Courtesy of the Banyan Tree Lijiang
Page 50 Michele Falzone/Age Fotostock
Pages 51 top, 51 bottom Courtesy of the Banyan Tree Lijiang
Pages 52, 53 Courtesy of the Uma by Como
Page 54 top Jimmy Tran/Shutterstock
Page 54 bottom Cristal Tran/Shutterstock
Page 55 Vidler Steve/Prisma/Age Fotostock
Page 56 top Aoshi VN/Shutterstock
Pages 56 bottom, 57 top, 57 bottom Courtesy of the The Nam Hai
Page 58 Luciano Lepre/Tips Images
Page 59 Kugler Jean/Prisma/Age Fotostock
Page 60 Kjersti Jørgensen/YAY Micro/Age Fotostock
Pages 61 top, 61 bottom Courtesy of the Belmond La Résidence Phou Vao
Page 62 top Livio Bourbon/Archivio White Star

Page 62 bottom Courtesy of the Raffles Grand Hotel d'Angkor
Page 63 Livio Bourbon/Archivio White Star
Pages 64 top, 64 bottom Courtesy of the Rayavadee
Page 65 apiguide/Shutterstock
Page 66 top konmesa/Shutterstock
Pages 66 bottom, 68, 69 top, 69 bottom Courtesy of the Dhara Dhevi
Page 67 Chatchai Somwat/Shutterstock
Page 70 Courtesy of the Belmond Road to Mandalay
Page 71 Bule Sky Studio/Shutterstock
Page 72 Blaine Harrington/Age Fotostock
Page 73 Jan Wlodarczyk/Age Fotostock
Page 74 top Milan Surkala/123rf
Pages 75 top, 75 bottom Courtesy of the The Oberoi Armavilas
Page 76 Marcello Libra/Archivio White Star
Page 77 Wendy Connett/Robert Harding Picture Library/Age Fotostock
Page 78 sergwsq/123rf
Pages 79 top, 79 bottom Courtesy of the Rambagh Palace
Page 80 Yadid Levy/Age Fotostock
Pages 81, 82 top Du Boisberranger Jean/Hemis.fr/Age Fotostock
Pages 82 bottom, 83 bottom Courtesy of the Kahanda Kanda
Page 83 top Stuart Pearce/Age Fotostock
Page 84 Courtesy of the Four Seasons Resort Maldives at Landaa Giraavaru
Page 85 top Josef Beck/imagebroker/Age Fotostock
Pages 85 bottom, 86, 86-87 Courtesy of the Four Seasons Resort Maldives at Landaa Giraavaru
Page 88 Courtesy of the One&Only Royal Mirage
Page 89 dblight/iStockphoto
Pages 90, 91 Marcello Libra/Archivio White Star
Page 92 Massimo Borchi/Archivio White Star
Pages 93 top, 93 bottom Courtesy of the Evason Ma'In Hot Springs, Six Senses Resort & Spa
Page 94 top Siegfried Kuttig/imagebroker/Age Fotostock
Page 94 bottom Courtesy of the Exclusive Gulets
Page 95 Siegfried imagesandstories/Blickwinkel/Age Fotostock
Page 96 top Schmid-Neebe Elke/Prisma/Age Fotostock
Page 96 bottom K Salminen/Blickwinkel/Age Fotostock
Page 97 JTB Photo/Age Fotostock
Pages 98, 99 top, 99 bottom Courtesy of the Ice Hotel
Page 100 top Galina Starintseva/123rf
Page 100 bottom Tatiana Savvateeva/123rf
Page 101 Tatiana Savvateeva/123rf
Page 102 top Sonnet Sylvain/Hemis.fr/Getty Images
Page 102 bottom Courtesy of the Hotel Astoria
Page 103 top sborisov/123rf
Page 103 bottom Zoonar/Kudrin Ruslan/Age Fotostock
Pages 104 top, 104 bottom, 105 Courtesy of the Juvet Landscape Hotel
Page 106 top Rafal Kwiatkowski/123rf
Page 106 bottom Courtesy of the Ardanaseig Hotel
Page 107 Rieger Bertrand/Hemis.fr/Age Fotostock

Page 108 ARCO/T Schäffer/Arco Images/Age Fotostock
Pages 108-109 Adam Burton/Robert Harding Picture Library/Age Fotostock
Page 110 top Moirenc Camille/Hemis.fr/Age Fotostock
Page 110 bottom Courtesy of the Château de Colombier
Page 111 ARCO/R. Kiedrowski/Arco Images/Age Fotostock
Page 112 ARCO/Scholz, F/Arco Images/Age Fotostock
Pages 112-113 JoselgnacioSoto/iStockphoto
Page 114 Stefano Scata'/Tips Images
Page 115 Sylvain Grandadam/Age Fotostock
Pages 116, 117 top, 117 bottom Courtesy of the Domaine Les Crayères
Page 118 top Yann Guichaoua/Age Fotostock
Page 118 bottom Funkystock/Age Fotostock
Page 119 Florian Monheim/Bildarchiv Monheim/Age Fotostock
Page 120 top Vidler Steve/TravelPix/Marka
Page 120 bottom Renault Philippe/Hemis.fr/Age Fotostock
Pages 121 top, 121 bottom Courtesy of the Château des Briottières
Page 122 top Noppasin Wongchum/123rf
Page 122 bottom Courtesy of the Das König Ludwig Hotel, Spa & Wellness
Page 123 Shen Tao/Shutterstock
Pages 124, 126 bottom lef Courtesy of the The Chedi Andermatt
Page 125 Massimo Pizzotti/Age Fotostock
Pages 126-127 P. Frischknecht/Arco Images/Age Fotostock
Page 126 top lef Anton J. Geisser
Pages 128-129 Pierre Jacques/Hemis.fr/Getty Images
Page 128 bottom AFP/Stringer/Getty Images
Pages 130 top, 130 bottom, 131 top, 131 bottom Courtesy of the Les Fermes de Marie
Page 132 Courtesy of the Cristallo Hotel, Spa & Golf
Page 133 Walter Zerla/Cubo Images
Pages 134-135 Katja Kreder/imagebroker/Age Fotostock
Page 135 Marcello Bertinetti
Page 136 Aleksandrs Kosarevs/123rf
Page 137 Marcello Bertinetti
Pages 138 top, 138 bottom, 139 top, 139 bottom Courtesy of the Hotel Danieli
Page 140 AlbertoSimonetti/iStockphoto
Page 141 Dudarev Mikhail/Shutterstock
Page 142 top argalis/iStockphoto
Page 142 bottom Lynne Otter/Age Fotostock
Page 143 top, 143 bottom Courtesy of the Byblos Art Hotel Villa Amistà
Pages 144 top, 144 bottom Courtesy of the Belmond Hotel Splendido e Splendido Mare
Page 145 Antonio Attini/Archivio White Star
Page 146 Stevan ZZ/Shutterstock
Page 147 top Jennifer Barrow/123rf
Page 147 bottom leoks/Shutterstock
Page 148 Courtesy of the La Colombe d'Or
Page 149 Sylvain Sonnet/Getty Images
Page 150 Andreas Karelias/123rf
Page 151 top OSOMEDIA/Age Fotostock
Page 151 bottom Gerth Roland/Prisma/Age Fotostock
Page 152 top Sergii Figurnyi/123rf

Page 152 bottom Antonio Attini/Archivio White Star
Page 153 Antonio Attini/Archivio White Star
Page 154 Tomas Marek/123rf
Pages 155 top, 155 bottom Courtesy of the Relais La Suvera
Pages 156 top, 156 bottom, 158-159, 158 top, 158 bottom Courtesy of the Belmond Hotel Caruso
Page 157 Anne Conway/Archivio White Star
Page 160 Courtesy of the Lešic Dimitri Palace
Page 161 Bertrand Gardel/Hemis.fr/Corbis
Page 162 top Alfio Garozzo/Archivio White Star
Page 162 bottom artubo/iStockphoto
Page 163 Courtesy of the Mystique Resort
Page 164 top Antonio Attini/Archivio White Star
Page 164 bottom Courtesy of the Hotel Alfonso XIII
Page 165 Antonio Attini/Archivio White Star
Page 166 top M&G Therin-Weise/Age Fotostock
Page 166 bottom Salva Garrigues/Age Fotostock
Page 167 Nick K/Shutterstock
Page 168 Rui Vale De Souse/123rf
Page 169 Gunter Hoffmann/123rf
Pages 170-171 Nicola Zingarelli/Moment Open/Getty Images
Pages 171 top, 171 bottom Courtesy of the Aldeia da Cuada
Page 172 top Karol Kozlowski/123rf
Page 172 bottom Courtesy of the Ksar Char-Bagh
Page 173 Urs Flueeler/Zoonar/Age Fotostock
Pages 174 top, 174 bottom, 175 Marcello Bertinetti
Pages 176 top, 176 bottom, 177 top, 177 bottom Dylan Chandler, Courtesy of the Nour el Nil
Pages 178 top, 178 bottom, 179, 181 Courtesy of the Frégate Island Private/Oetker Collection
Pages 180-181 Cornelia Doerr/Getty Images
Page 182 top Frans Lanting/National Geographic Creative
Page 182 bottom Michael Poliza/National Geographic Creative
Page 183 Bill Bachmann/Age Fotostock
Page 184 top Adam Jones/Getty Images
Page 184 bottom Dustie/Shutterstock
Pages 185 top, 185 bottom Courtesy of the Cottar's 1920s Camp
Page 186 Hector Conesa/123rf
Page 187 Suzi Eszterhas/Minden Pictures/National Geographic Creative
Pages 188 top, 188 bottom, 189 top, 189 bottom Courtesy of the Singita Serengeti
Pages 190 top, 190 bottom, 191, 192, 193 top, 193 bottom Courtesy of the Constance Tsarabanjina Resort
Pages 194 top, 194 bottom Courtesy of the Le Touessrok
Page 195 Iconodec/Alamy/IPA
Page 196, 197, 198 Courtesy of the Royal Livingstone Hotel
Page 199 John Warburton-Lee/Getty Images
Page 200 Niels van Gijn/JAI/Corbis
Pages 201 top, 201 bottom Courtesy of the Dana Allen/Little Mombo Camp

Page 202 top Sergio Pitamitz/Hemis.fr/Corbis
Page 202 bottom Courtesy of the Dana Allen/Little Mombo Camp
Pages 203 top, 203 bottom Courtesy of the Dana Allen/Little Mombo Camp
Page 204 top Michelle Sole/Shutterstock
Pages 204 top, 205 Courtesy of the Sabi Sabi Private Game Reserve
Pages 206 top, 206 bottom, 207 McPhoto/IQ Images/Age Fotostock
Pages 208 top, 208 bottom, 209 top, 209 bottom Courtesy of the Dunes Lodge (Wolwedans Collection)/NamibRand Safaris
Page 210 top Wave Royalty Free/Age Fotostock
Page 210 bottom Courtesy of the Nita Lake Lodge
Page 211 John Pitcher/iStockphoto
Pages 212 top, 212 bottom, 213 Courtesy of the The Resort at Paws Up
Page 214 top jovannig/Kalium/Age Fotostock
Page 214 bottom Courtesy of the The Wauwinet
Page 215 Raymond Forbes/Age Fotostock
Page 216 John Greim/Age Fotostock
Pages 216-217 Jihan Abdalla
Page 218 top Jared Ropelato/Shutterstock
Page 218 bottom Courtesy of the Kodiak Greenwood/Cavallo Point
Page 219 fcarucci/iStockphoto
Pages 220 top, 220 bottom Courtesy of the Kodiak Greenwood/Cavallo Point
Page 221 Andrew Zarivny/123rf
Page 222 top phbcz/iStockphoto
Page 222 bottom Courtesy of the Moab Under Canvas
Page 223 Doug Meek/Shutterstock
Page 224 lightpix/iStockphoto
Pages 224-225 Francesco R. Iacomino/Shutterstock
Page 226 top Henryk Sadura/Tetra Images/Age Fotostock
Page 226 bottom Kord.com/Age Fotostock
Page 227 Richard Ellis/Age Fotostock
Page 228 top Dave Allen Photography/Shutterstock
Page 228 bottom Blaine Harrington III/Corbis
Pages 229 top, 229 bottom Courtesy of the Wentworth Mansion/Charming Inns
Page 230 top Courtesy of the Little Palm Island Resort & Spa
Page 230 bottom Kord.com/Age Fotostock
Page 231 Tom Stack/WaterFram/Age Fotostock
Page 232 Image Source/Getty Images
Pages 232-233 David Doubilet/National Geographic Creative
Page 234 top Sorin Colac/123rf
Page 234 bottom Courtesy of the Las Ventanas al Paraiso
Page 235 Christopher Swann/Specialist Stock RM/Age Fotostock
Pages 236 top, 236 bottom Courtesy of the Edgardo Contreras/L'Otel San Miguel de Allende
Page 237 Craig Lovell/Ramble/Age Fotostock
Page 238 top Massimo Borchi/Archivio White Star
Page 238 bottom Courtesy of the Hacienda Temozón

Page 239 Antonio Attini/Archivio White Star
Page 240 top Bobby Haas/National Geographic Creative
Page 240 bottom Olivera Rusu per Cayo Espanto - www.aprivateisland.com
Page 241 Norbert Probst/imagebroker/Age Fotostock
Pages 242-243 Juan Carlos Muñoz/Age Fotostock
Page 244 Ramunas Bruzas/Shutterstock
Pages 245 top, 245 bottom Courtesy of the One&Only Ocean Club
Page 246 top Doug Pearson/JAI/Corbis
Page 246 bottom Alvaro Leiva/Age Fotostock
Page 247 Courtesy of the Round Hill Hotel & Villas
Page 248 Peter Phipp/Age Fotostock
Page 249, 251 top, 251 bottom Courtesy of the Sea Cloud Cruises/Hansa Treuhand Group
Page 250 top Neil Emmerson/Robert Harding Picture Library/Age Fotostock
Page 250 bottom Norbert Probst/imagebroker/Age Fotostock
Page 252 top Edwin Giesbers/naturepl.com/BlueGreen
Pages 252 bottom, 253 Courtesy of the Pacuare Lodge
Page 254 Pete Oxford/Minden Pictures/National Geographic
Page 255 Danita Delimont Stock/Age Fotostock
Pages 256, 257 top, 257 bottom Courtesy of the La Selva Amazon Ecolodge & Spa
Page 258 top Antonio Attini/Archivio White Star
Page 258 bottom Courtesy of the La Casona/Inkaterra
Page 259 Danita Delimont Stock/Age Fotostock
Pages 260, 261 Courtesy of the Piero Zolin/Uxua Casa Hotel & Spa
Pages 262 top, 262 bottom Courtesy of the Alto Atacama Desert Lodge & Spa
Page 263 holgs/iStockphoto
Page 264 top Alfio Garozzo/Archivio White Star
Page 264 bottom Courtesy of the El Calafate Design Suites
Page 265 Pichugin Dimitri/Shutterstock

Cover
One&Only Hayman Island - Inner Reef Langford Island
Courtesy of the One&Only Hayman Island.
Photographer: Simon Upton

Back cover
Top: Lapland / Sweden
Courtesy of the Ice Hotel

Center, left: Champagne / France
Courtesy of the Domaine Les Crayères

Center, right: Chiang Mai / Thailand
Courtesy of the Dhara Dhevi

Bottom, left: Maasai Mara / Kenya
Courtesy of the Cottar's 1920s Camp

Bottom, right: Sunnmøre Alps / Norway
Courtesy of the Juvet Landscape Hotel

WHITE STAR PUBLISHERS

WS White Star Publishers® is a registered trademark property of De Agostini Libri S.p.A.

© 2014 De Agostini Libri S.p.A.
Via G. da Verrazano, 15 - 28100 Novara, Italy - www.whitestar.it - www.deagostini.it

Translation: Richard Pierce

ISBN 978-88-544-0844-9
1 2 3 4 5 6   18 17 16 15 14

Printed in China